COMMUNICATION
& INTERACTION
IN THE EARLY YEARS

SAGE was founded in 1965 by Sara Miller McCune to support the dissemination of usable knowledge by publishing innovative and high-quality research and teaching content. Today, we publish more than 850 journals, including those of more than 300 learned societies, more than 800 new books per year, and a growing range of library products including archives, data, case studies, reports, and video. SAGE remains majority-owned by our founder, and after Sara's lifetime will become owned by a charitable trust that secures our continued independence.

Los Angeles | London | New Delhi | Singapore | Washington DC

COMMUNICATION
& INTERACTION
IN THE EARLY YEARS

Ann Clare

Los Angeles | London | New Delhi
Singapore | Washington DC

Los Angeles | London | New Delhi
Singapore | Washington DC

SAGE Publications Ltd
1 Oliver's Yard
55 City Road
London EC1Y 1SP

SAGE Publications Inc.
2455 Teller Road
Thousand Oaks, California 91320

SAGE Publications India Pvt Ltd
B 1/I 1 Mohan Cooperative Industrial Area
Mathura Road
New Delhi 110 044

SAGE Publications Asia-Pacific Pte Ltd
3 Church Street
#10-04 Samsung Hub
Singapore 049483

Editor: Amy Jarrold
Assistant editor: George Knowles
Production editor: Tom Bedford
Copyeditor: Andy Baxter
Proofreader: David Hemsley
Marketing manager: Dilhara Attygalle
Cover design: Wendy Scott
Typeset by: C&M Digitals (P) Ltd, Chennai, India
Printed and bound by CPI Group (UK) Ltd,
Croydon, CR0 4YY

Library of Congress Control Number: 2015939587

British Library Cataloguing in Publication data

A catalogue record for this book is available from
the British Library

ISBN 978–1-4739-0676-1
ISBN 978–1-4739-0677-8 (pbk)

Contents

About the author

Ann Clare began her career as a secondary school English teacher. It was after having her three children, Felicity, Edward and Hannah, that she became the head of a small village private nursery school at the same time as studying for her Master's degree. Ann followed this by becoming an Early Years Consultant working for two North West local authorities.

A chance conversation with Professor Cathy Nutbrown encouraged her to further her studies at the University of Sheffield where she graduated with her PhD, researching babies and young children under three.

This research led Ann on to write her first book, *Creating a Learning Environment for Babies and Toddlers* in 2012, and to co-author a second edition of *Working with Babies and Toddlers* with Jools Page and Cathy Nutbrown in 2013.

The arrival of Ann's two grandchildren, Oscar and Lottie, further inspired her to write this new book focusing on interaction and communication in the early years. Ann is now enjoying a happy retirement which is filled with her continued work with the University of Sheffield, making bread and visiting her gorgeous grandchildren in Germany.

Acknowledgements

As always I am indebted to those who have helped in the writing of this book: Finley Newton for his wonderful letters, Ruth Holland and Sam.

Thanks go to Amy Jarrold for her enthusiasm which has kept me going throughout.

The young people in my life continue to inspire me: Fliss, Edd and Hannah for all their youthful memories, Oscar for being the stimulus behind this book and Lottie for continuing to surprise me.

Lastly I want to dedicate this book to the most wonderful story teller and father, James Hilton Brownlow, CBE, QPM; I miss you. Thank you daddy.

List of figures and tables

Figures

Tables

Setting the scene

1

This chapter will:

- Discuss the development of the early years curriculum since 2000
- Give a broad overview of the Rose Review on literacy
- Reflect on the position of settings within the private sector
- Discuss the challenges of two year olds' language development

One of the things that separates us from the rest of the animal world is our ability to communicate through the written and spoken word, so it is understandable that these skills are high in the social and political policy and practice for early years.

Curriculum Guidance for the Foundation Stage and birth-to-three matters

Since the introduction of the *Curriculum Guidance for the Foundation Stage* (CGFS) in 2000 (DfES, 2000) early years development and practice has been high on the government agenda. Since the introduction of the CGFS various governments have looked at children's development to identify areas of learning where children are failing to make appropriate progress; especially when compared to international outcomes.

Before we become embroiled in statistical data and political argument we need to look more closely at policy documentation that has evolved during the recent past.

The publication of the CGFS in 2000 left a gaping hole in early years documentation when it failed to address the learning and development needs of children under the age of three. As with previous publications and research the CGFS gave the impression that learning only takes place once a child has reached the age of three. Under the leadership of the great ambassador for early years, Lesley Abbott, this lack of guidance for under threes was addressed with the introduction of *Birth to Three Matters* (B23) (DfES, 2002). This document sought to give support to professionals working with very small children, recognising the amazing development that takes place before and after birth:

> Babies come already designed, or programmed, to be deeply interested in the people and world in which they find themselves. They learn best by playing with things they find in their world, and above all by playing with the familiar people who love them. (David et al., 2003, p. 150)

With the arrival of B23 the learning needs of babies and very young children were becoming part of the early years agenda. Work on brain development (Gopnik, 1999) showed that even before birth babies are 'programmed' to learn and communicate. At last government policy was looking at a top-up rather than a top-down model of development, but if this longitudinal look at learning within human beings was to be consistent then the policy had to become unified. It was then that the Early Years Foundation Stage (EYFS) (DCSF, 2008, a, b,c) was introduced which for the first time looked at babies' and young children's learning and development from birth to five years of age. This document saw that babies and children do not develop according to static ages and stages of development but rather that children can reach stages at different times. This was recognised in the way in which the Curriculum Guidance (DCSF, 2008a, b) looked at overlapping age bands. The statutory framework stated that

> Children are competent learners from birth and develop and learn in a wide variety of ways. All practitioners should, therefore, look carefully at the children in their care, consider their needs, their interests, and their stages of development and use all of this information to help plan a challenging and enjoyable experience across all the areas of Learning and Development. (DCSF, 2008c, p. 11)

Early Years Foundation Stage

The EYFS of 2008 was superseded by the revised EYFS in 2012 after the review, *The Early Years: Foundations for Life, Health and Learning*, led by Clare Tickell (2011). This document was a slimmed down version of the original EYFS and to a certain extent introduced a different tone of voice from the coalition government, with the introduction of the concept of school readiness, where

> The three prime areas reflect the key skills and capacities all children need to develop and learn effectively, and become ready for school. (DfE, 2012b, p. 6)

> As children grow older and approach five, the balance should shift towards a more equal focus across all of the prime and specific areas, progressively adapting to a child's developing capabilities and interests, but always ensuring that any child whose progress in the prime areas gives cause for concern receives the support they need. (DfE, 2012b, p. 27)

The revised EYFS also offered non-statutory guidance for practitioners in the document *Development Matters* developed by Early Education (2012). The EYFS of 2012 was again revised for implementation in September 2014 though these revisions were largely related to childminders and safeguarding.

Once the policy documents were in place the government turned its attention to look more closely at why some children were failing to meet targets at later stages of their education.

Government reviews

Part of this deeper examination resulted in the reviews by Graham Allen and Ian Duncan-Smith, *Early Intervention: Good Parents, Great Kids, Better Citizens* (2008); Frank Field, *The Foundation Years: Preventing Poor Children Becoming Poor Adults* (2010); and Graham Allen, *Early Intervention: The Next Steps* (2011). In these reviews the issue of early identification was highlighted as a driver for improving some of the outcomes:

> it is not surprising that Early Intervention to provide young children with what they need carries many positive effects that cascade through their future lives and into the lives of those around them. (Allen and Duncan-Smith, 2008, p. 67)

As a result of this cross-party research the government began to introduce funding for two year olds. Much in the same way that nursery education funding was introduced for three year olds, funding for two year olds was targeted at those children who were seen as disadvantaged. As with three year old funding, the new funding system, while essentially about raising the aspirations of disadvantaged two year olds was also about the political agenda of getting mothers back into the work place in an endeavour to break the cycle of children being raised in workless families.

At the same time, and in line with Allen's *Early Identification* review (2011), the two year old progress check was introduced as part of the revised EYFS of 2012; it is a review of child development, health and readiness for school at two to two-and-a-half years. Although the check was statutory the government gave settings the freedom to meet the require-ments in their own way. Support was offered in the form of guidance developed by the National Children's Bureau (DfE, 2014c).

The framework stated that

> This progress check must identify the child's strengths, and any areas where the child's progress is less than expected. If there are significant emerging concerns, or an identified special educational need or disability, practitioners should develop a targeted plan to support the child's future learning and development involving other professionals (for example, the provider's Special Educational Needs Co-ordinator) as appropriate. (DfE, 2012b, p. 10)

The check has to be completed when a child is between 24 and 36 months and is to be shared with parents. It is to report mainly on a child's progress within the three Prime Areas of Learning. The idea is that this report on a child's learning development is looked at along with the two year old health check which is carried out by health visitors when a child has reached their second birthday. In many local authorities there is a move for these two checks to be completed at the same time and in partnership so that parents have a complete picture of their child's development. For example, for the Health Visitor to conduct their checks in the setting so that there truly is a compre-hensive overview of a child's emotional, physical and language development with all parties, parents, health and setting contributing. This is an ideal model but in practical terms this is sometimes strategically difficult. For example, par-ents do not necessarily send their children to settings in close proximity to their homes (Clare, 2012) and Health Visitors are constrained by authority areas.

The development of the Early Years Foundation Stage

The EYFS of 2012 also placed an emphasis on the 'Characteristics of Effective Learning', giving practitioners the opportunity to look at how young children's emotional well-being impacts on their ability to develop a disposition for learning, as well as the individual ways in which children learn through their play.

Another change within the revised EYFS was that made to the areas of learning. In the original EYFS equal weighting was given to the following six areas of learning, and all were to be delivered through planned, purposeful play, with a balance of adult-led and child-initiated activities.

- **Personal Social and Emotional development (PSE)** including Dispositions and Attitudes, Positive Relationships, Self-care, Sense of Community
- **Communication Language and Literacy (CLL)** including Language for Communication, Language for Thinking, Linking Sounds and Letters, Reading, Writing, Handwriting
- **Problem Solving Reasoning and Numeracy (PSRN)** including Numbers as Labels and for Counting, Calculating, Shape, Space and Measures
- **Knowledge and Understanding of the World (KUW)** including Exploration and Investigation, Designing and Making, Information and Communications Technology, Time, Place, Communities
- **Physical Development (PD)** including Movement and Space, Health and Bodily Awareness, Using Equipment and Materials
- **Creative development (CD)** including Being Creative – Responding to Experiences, Expressing and Communicating Ideas, Exploring Media and Materials, Creating Music and Dance, Developing Imagination and Imaginative Play

In the revised edition some of the areas of learning were renamed and three of the areas were given predominance and became known as the Prime Areas of Learning, with the remainder known as the Specific Areas.

Prime Areas

- **Communication and Language (CL)** including
  - o Communication Language
  - o Listening and Attention
  - o Speaking

- **Physical Development (PD)** including
  - o Moving and Handling
  - o Health and Self-care

- **Personal, Social and Emotional Development (PSE)** including
  - Self-confidence and Self-awareness
  - Managing Feelings and Behaviour
  - Making Relationships

Specific Areas

- **Literacy** including
  - Reading and Writing
- **Mathematics** including
  - Numbers
  - Shape, Space and Measures
- **Understanding the World** including
  - People and Communities
  - The World
  - Technology
- **Expressive Arts and Design** including
  - Exploring and Using Media and Materials
  - Being Imaginative

The establishment of the three Prime Areas of Learning recognised the impact that physical, personal, social and emotional, and language development has on the overall development of children. Without progress being made in these three areas of learning children are at a disadvantage.

This can be seen in the Prime Area of Communication and Language; the ability for children to communicate through the medium of speech is the basis for much of children's later holistic development. Without language acquisition children find it difficult to make progress in other 'academic' areas of learning.

When children begin to be able to talk with their peers and adults in an understandable way, then many of the frustrations that are often called the 'terrible twos' are alleviated. Such frustration can be seen again in older sections of our society where dementia causes much disturbance, as making oneself understood again becomes a problem. Children, to ease their frustrations, develop strategies to overcome this difficulty – developing ways to communicate through gesture.

Alternative communication systems

Many young children today are introduced to formal systems of signing such as Signalong (www.signalong.org.uk/methodology/index.htm), which is a sign-supported communication method introduced in 1992 for people with communication difficulties mostly associated with learning disabilities, autism and other special needs, and which is based on British Sign Language. This system appears to have some impact on the frustrations of young children that can often lead to behavioural issues.

Just as Signalong was developed to support children with learning difficulties so was the system of Picture Exchange Communication (PECS) which was developed in 1985 'as a unique augmentative/alternative communication intervention package for individuals with autism spectrum disorder and related developmental disabilities'.

PECS begins by teaching an individual to give a picture of a desired item to a 'communicative partner' who immediately honours the exchange as a request. The system goes on to teach discrimination of pictures and how to put them together in sentences. In the more advanced phases, individuals are taught to answer questions and to comment (www.pecs-unitedkingdom. com/pecs.php).

In order to encourage communication skills through other means than vocalisations a system called Baby Signing has been introduced, which has become very popular with parents who are interested in having more communication with their babies. I have worked with settings where this system of signing has been used very successfully but there are many who question its validity and worth, 'Although Baby Sign is gaining in popularity, there is a scarcity of research supporting its use. The research that has been conducted is conflicting' (Mueller et al., 2013).

Along with policy development within the curriculum the government have also seen the need to introduce 'packages' to support practitioners in delivering high quality interaction in their exchanges with children. One of the first of many such strategies was the *Communication Matters* (DfES, 2005) training which was an extended training for teachers and practitioners to help them look closely and challenge their ways of interacting with and encouraging language in young children. Through the use of video clips and practical tasks this training demonstrated how, as practitioners, we all tend to crowd children's talking spaces under the misapprehension that what we have to say is empowering children in their language, whereas in fact we are inhibiting the young child's ability to communicate because there is limited space within which to do this. As a local authority consultant I have delivered this training on many occasions and have found that it has benefitted practitioners and challenged them to rethink how they interact.

The Primary National Strategies also introduced a range of materials for practitioners to support children's language and communication development:

- Every Child a Talker (ECAT) (in 2009)
- Communication, Language and Literacy Development (CLLD) programme: Materials for practitioners (in 2008)
- Mark Making Matters: Young children making meaning in all areas of learning and development (in 2008)
- Inclusion Development Programme: Supporting children with speech, language and communication needs: Guidance for practitioners in the Early Years Foundation Stage (in 2008)
- Supporting children learning English as an additional language: Guidance for practitioners in the Early Years Foundation Stage (in 2007)
- Communication, Language and Literacy: Professional development resource (in 2007)

With all this guidance and support it is surprising that some of the statistical data from the OECD (2014) shows that children in the UK are not making the appropriate progress in their development in communication and, as a consequence, in their development in the associated areas of reading and writing. So with this plethora of information, why are we greeted by headlines showing that for our 15 year old children we are not making progress in reading and that the gap between the genders in the UK is larger than in other countries (OECD, 2014)? In his comments to the House of Commons, Michael Gove (Hansard, 2013) talked about what implications these results have for our youngest children, and what initiatives need to be put in place to change this situation. Along with the increased funding for disadvantaged two year olds to access early years education, in line with the recommendations of Field (2010) and Allen (2011), he also discussed one of the initiatives introduced by the coalition government as a driver for improvement:

> In our drive to eliminate illiteracy, we have introduced a screening check at age six to make sure that every child is reading fluently. (Hansard, 2013)

Will this screening be a true reflection of where a child's literacy development is? What the phonics screening, introduced in 2012, does not do is assess whether children have a love of books and therefore want to read and see the importance of understanding the written word. What it also does not do is assess or measure children's communication skills. Arguably, what the phonics screening does do is to challenge the professional ability of teachers to assess where children are and also put pressure on some of our youngest children to 'perform to the test'.

Elizabeth Truss was right when she argued, 'It's about developing the language, communication and social skills so that children are ready to learn when they are at school', as well as pointing out that 'At the moment, there is an 18 month vocabulary gap between children on low incomes and children on high incomes when they arrive at school' (Truss, 2014). When the OECD discuss the curricula of countries they show that it is those countries that assess children shortly after they enter primary education where they see that the most focus is placed on literacy and numeracy (OECD, 2012). Their analysis states that, 'Literacy has also been consistently linked to improved school performance and achievement as well as higher productivity later in life' (OECD, 2012, p. 86). This view is supported by research and to a certain extent is unchallengeable, but for me it is how we go about this that is the most important factor.

The EYFS of 2012 looked at the holistic development of children, identifying Communication and Language as one of the Prime Areas, with Literacy (and its focus on reading and writing) as a specific area of learning and development. What perhaps needs to be considered is whether some of the changes in government language (for example, *Development Matters* (Early Education, 2012) changed to *Early Years Outcomes* (DfE, 2013b)), by inference suggest that it is the outcome rather than the process which is of greater importance. The OECD (2012) unpicks development and language to state that, 'Evidence suggests literacy should focus on improving vocabulary and listening skills; building knowledge of the alphabetic code; and introduce printing' (p. 86).

The Rose Review

In June 2005 Jim Rose was asked to head up a review on literacy. In his summary Rose comments on the importance of listening and speaking skills in the early years as he sees these along with reading and writing as the 'prime communication skills that are central to children's intellectual, social and emotional development' (Rose, 2006, p. 3). It was through the publication of this review that synthetic phonics was seen as the next step to build upon the achievements recorded as a result of the National Literacy Strategy (NLS), which advocated a structured teaching programme within the primary education system. For many in the teaching profession the NLS was seen as too constricting, giving teachers limited opportunities to develop their children's reading skills at a pace relevant to their individual development – something which is one of the core principles within early years pedagogy. Although generally the NLS was seen as successful.

The Rose review sought to build on it with the message that phonics should be introduced to children before they start compulsory statutory education, when it is deemed a child is ready to move on in their communication and language development (Rose, 2006, p. 3).

The concerns raised in the review about the standards of teaching and learning, especially in relation to boys as they progressed through the education system, and the subsequent analysis of data, led the government to see a need for children to have more phonic knowledge and skill.

The following case study gives an example of how a boy aged three is demonstrating signs that he is ready for the next level.

Case study

Oscar is three years old and is a competent speaker in both English and German. He has recently begun to demonstrate an interest in letters and what they mean. As with all children he makes connections with the letter shapes and sounds within his own experiences. So building on this interest, and through support from his parents, Oscar is able to recognise the initial sounds and letter shape of his own name. He is interested then in the shape and sounds of the names of those around him. This is evidenced by the local German shop called D&M which Oscar refers to as the Mummy and Daddy shop.

This brief picture of Oscar shows that he is perhaps ready to have his interest challenged, to have his learning scaffolded by a skilled and knowledgeable adult in a Vygotskian (1978) manner, to move his knowledge and understanding of letter shapes and sounds forwards.

Activity

Consider how as a practitioner you might extend Oscar's learning of letter shapes and sounds. This might include his exposure to and recognition of environmental print in its many forms.

Whilst acknowledging in the review teachers' comments about not having a 'one size fits all' model, Rose (2006) is adamant that phonics should be taught in short discrete daily sessions with pace, which entails working with a best fit for the majority of children. Rose does not, however, see that phonics is the whole picture but a part of the fuller picture, as this book will demonstrate.

> Although this review focuses upon phonic work, it is very important to understand what the rest of the picture looks like and requires. For example, nurturing positive attitudes to literacy and the skills associated with them, across the curriculum, is crucially important as is developing spoken language, building vocabulary, grammar, comprehension and facility with ICT. (Rose, 2006, p. 16)

So what were the recommendations with regard to synthetic phonics? Perhaps a good starting point is to define what is meant by this term:

- grapheme/phoneme (letter/sound) correspondences (the alphabetic principle) in a clearly defined, incremental sequence
- to apply the highly important skill of blending (synthesising) phonemes in order, all through a word to read it
- to apply the skills of segmenting words into their constituent phonemes to spell
- that blending and segmenting are reversible processes (Rose, 2006, p. 20)

Rose saw that once programmes were adopted they were diminished if implemented with a mix-and-match approach. He identified the following as the most salient features of any system and the manner in which it should be taught:

1. Fast paced
2. Careful and consistent
3. Well planned
4. Multi-sensory
5. Based on sound assessment and tracking across all four strands of literacy
6. Teaching letter names as well as sounds
7. Good enunciation of the sounds by the teacher
8. The use of 'real books' to complement and strengthen a programme

With regard to the pedagogy and practice of the early years Rose supported the practice of embedding children's early literacy skills of communication within the EYFS, stating that the skills needed for future phonics work should be deeply rooted in the environment and across all areas of learning as part of a language-rich curriculum. (This concept will be further explored throughout this book, looking at the ways in which the environment and the curriculum can ensure that children have the skills necessary for phonic work when they enter full time education.) This was meant to alleviate fears that teaching within the early years would become formalised and that children would be introduced to phonics at too early a stage of their development.

The Rose Review was the precursor to how reading and writing and the necessary skills for children to become effective readers and writers have now become embedded within the curriculum. One of the offshoots from this review was the introduction of *Letters and Sounds* (DfES, 2007) and the *Every Child a Talker* (DCSF, 2008b) programme which will be discussed in the following chapters in relation to the relevant ages and stages of development.

The workforce

Much of our focus so far has been on the government policy agenda, which is as it should be, for in order to know where we are going we have to know where we have come from. Government is the driver of policy which affects us all; it has long been agreed that early years is the foundation on which to build the future generations and there has been much criticism of the workforce and its ability to deliver high quality teaching and learning when its level of qualifications is so low. Nutbrown (DfE, 2012a) sought to address this issue in the government commissioned review of the early years work force, but as her reaction to the government response to her findings demonstrates, not all of her recommendations were taken forward:

> Why? Because, as they say, 'the devil is in the detail' … As I read beyond the headlines of the government proposals I realised that most of my recommendations had in effect been rejected. (Nutbrown, 2013, p. 2)

If Rose (2006) was talking about improving some of the low quality of teaching in the primary system, where all teachers are graduates, to deliver high quality practice, then surely this is something which still has to be addressed in the private sector where pay and conditions do not encourage the recruitment of graduate practitioners. Since the concept of an early years curriculum came into being there has been an upward trend in the quality and level of training but this still does not apply across the board.

When looking at the training of teachers and practitioners in relation to supporting the development of children's communication and language skills then it is apposite to look at the evaluations of specific programmes that have set out to do this. In the I CAN Early Talk (ET) programme the evaluation included the impact on the training of all those involved; parents, children and practitioners. When looking at practitioners working within Children's Centres the report stated that there were

> indications of a professional learning community forming around speech, language and communication (SLC), as ET and other initiatives were embedded. The formation of these communities supported a much deeper understanding of, and reflection on, SLC by practitioners. (Whitmarsh et al., 2011, p. 3)

The evaluation of this programme demonstrated that the upskilling of practitioners and teachers had a positive impact on children's communication and language.

Macrory (2010) discusses the vital importance of practitioners having a sound knowledge and understanding of the ways in which children acquire language. In his conclusion he goes so far as to suggest that

> If we really want to develop children's language, and to understand the part played by adults, other children and social contexts in their language development, then we should be arguing for an expert in language development in every early years setting. (Macrory, 2010, p. 39)

If teachers and practitioners are important, more so are the input and support of parents. In the early years sector we glibly talk about parents being 'a child's first educator' but how much attention do we pay to this?

Questions for reflection

1. How do you ensure that what parents tell you about their child's cognitive development feeds into the child's assessments?
2. How do we truly build up partnerships where parents are valued?
3. How do we empower parents so that they can challenge children's communication skills?
4. How do we inform parents about best practice?
5. How do we dispel parental focus on reading to the detriment of the skills needed prior to learning how to read?

As an Early Years Foundation Stage Profile (EYFSP) moderator for local authorities since the profile became statutory, I have over the years seen the concern of some teachers about the levels of language that children come into either nursery or reception class with; and this is true across the spectrum, from settings where there was social deprivation to those where the children were of professional parents. However, when I ask specifically why practitioners think there has been a downward trend in the levels of language when children first enter school the answers I receive are varied and in some cases very surprising. In the deprived areas, there were issues around children who were coming in with no English, and around those who had had no experiences outside of the home from which to develop their social communication. With the children from professional families, suggested causes included being cared for by au pairs, whose personal aim is to work whilst learning English for themselves, and that children had limited human interaction because they spent too much time using digital media in one form or another.

If these are the issues, then throughout this book we need to ask ourselves not only how we can change this, but what do practitioners and teachers do the world over, for example, to empower children to become bilingual and to engage with printed as well as digital media?

In the ever-changing world of education there have been many who have expressed concerns about the way in which there is a top-down pressure on early years. This was evidenced in the Cambridge Review Report (Alexander, 2009) when it discussed the early starting age for schooling in the UK and argued that

> too formal too soon can be dangerously counterproductive. In 14 of the 15 countries that scored higher than England in a major study of reading and literacy in 2006, children did not enter school until they were six or seven. And more children read for pleasure in most of those countries than do so in England. (p. 16)

This report challenged the education system that we have today as being too formal whilst recognising that

> there can be no doubt whatsoever that literacy and numeracy are fundamental to primary education. But we must be able to extend their scope beyond reading, writing and arithmetic and to ask what, in the 21st century, is truly 'basic' to young children's education. (p. 18)

The issues surrounding the use of technology and how it can possibly support children's communication and literacy development will be discussed in subsequent chapters.

Conclusion

Much of the policy documentation around communication discussed so far has involved the maintained education system and is linked to children's reading and writing development, but in this book I am keen to explore what language development means for our very youngest children. In the next chapter we will look closely at how language develops from birth; but before we move out of the policy we need to look at how well prepared private day care provision is to meet the communication needs of the children in their care. Many settings today employ graduates but, as Nutbrown (DfE, 2012a) states, there are not enough of them. In her review for the government she states that evidence

> shows that highly qualified teams of early years practitioners are more effective in developing children's communication, language and literacy, reasoning, thinking and mathematical skills. (p. 15)

So why then are the graduates who work in the private sector still not given the same recognition as that given to those who have *qualified teacher status* (QTS)? The numbers of graduates in the private sector are still low, due to poor pay and working conditions, and therefore much of the work done with our very youngest children is carried out by non-graduates. This is not to denigrate the professionalism of those working in the early years nor the wealth of high quality experience that exists, but it is to say that adults working with young children need to know and have confidence in how they communicate and interact. Both Rose (2006) and Nutbrown (DfE, 2012a) recognised the need for high quality teachers and practitioners to support young children's language development, so it is imperative that the private sector focuses its attention on upskilling its workers so that they all give children quality communication and interaction.

The scene is now set for how we in the UK are striving to improve the levels of literacy of children; we will be looking at the ways in which the skills needed to become a proficient reader can be grounded in early years pedagogy, thus ensuring that the principles, practices and beliefs of early years philosophy and ethos are not compromised into a formal, structured way of learning that is too much too soon.

Questions for reflection

Considering the plethora of policy documentation since 2000 surrounding the early years sector, reflect on how you adhere to your personal and professional principles, values and beliefs when it comes to babies' and young children's communication.

Further reading

- Alexander, R. (2009) *Children, their World, their Education: Final Report and Recommendations of the Cambridge Primary Review.* Abingdon: Routledge.

Although the findings from the Cambridge Review did not find their place within government policy this is an interesting and sometimes controversial look at the UK primary curriculum.

- Rose, J. (2006) *Independent Review of the Teaching of Early Reading: Final Report.* Nottingham: DfES.

The Rose Review is an important document because of its influence on the way in which synthetic phonics has established its position within the teaching of reading within the UK primary education system.

- Mueller, V., Sepulveda, A. and Rodriguez, S. (2014) 'The effects of Baby Sign training on child development', *Early Child Development and Care*, 184: 1178–91.

In a contentious area of communication this article looks at the use of Baby Signing through a study of nine families with children ranging in age from six months to two years and five months who participated in a Baby Sign workshop. The data discussed suggests that the Baby Sign training had a significant, positive impact on the overall development of the children.

Early communication

2

This chapter will:

- Discuss the early communication of very young babies
- Examine the role of parents in their child's early communication
- Consider the importance of attachment and emotional well-being

The study of how children develop language is complex and it wasn't until the work of Brown and Hanlon (1970) and Chomsky (2003) that research demonstrated a rigorous and thorough understanding of the subject. Chomsky firmly believed that much of a child's language is genetically determined. He was of the opinion that language is acquired as opposed to something which is learned. There are many who would dispute this opinion when it comes down to the nature–nurture debate. What is it that makes a child an English speaker as opposed to a Chinese speaker; what is it that creates this difference when all human babies are basically born the same? There has been much research and discussion about critical or sensitive periods for language development (Lenneberg, 1967) and although it was strongly felt that language development took place between the ages of three and puberty there has been much controversy, resulting in Saxton's (2010) statement that 'the offset of any critical period – the point at which sensitivity starts to decline – must be more like five years, not the early teens, since most of the basic grammar we acquire is in place by age five' (p. 53).

Babies are born to communicate from the moment of their birth; they need to communicate with the wider world to tell adults what their needs are. They do this by crying. Frequently parents, mothers in particular, will talk about understanding their baby's particular cries (Clare, 2012). Given this innate impulse to communicate, it is important that practitioners understand the importance of their role in modelling language through the range of first-hand experiences that they offer to these early communicators.

With this innate ability to communicate, it is imperative that practitioners understand how to develop and challenge this impulse in meaningful ways. It is interesting to note that all babies from around the world have the ability to babble an international language. It is only through the exposure of listening to their 'mother' tongue' that the sounds that are not heard are pruned because they are not needed, 'the period between 6–12 months of age is when babies lose their ability to recognise sounds not used in their own particular language' (Robinson, 2003, p. 20). We have all marvelled at the ability of young children to accommodate a new and second language when they are exposed to sounds that are not present in their first language, and have been embarrassed at our adult attempts at acquiring another language. This example clearly illustrates the need for parents/ carers and practitioners to be very aware of their crucial role in exposing these developing minds to a range of experiences so that the children's brains can make the neural connections (Robinson, 2003).

When we consider the language of babies at birth and compare this to the language of a five year old it is apparent that in a short space of time the development is enormous – from the baby who uses cries to communicate their needs to the young child who can make their needs known, as well as being capable of holding a very sophisticated and complex conversation. This development is amazing as it appears that for the normally developing child this progress is natural.

In his book on child language, Saxton (2010) looks at the four main strands of language – phonology, vocabulary, morphology and syntax – and how these develop in the young child. He believes that babies do not just acquire these in separate stages but rather they are interdependent on one another. As he states, 'if we looked only at that [syntax], we would fail to notice that the child is simultaneously learning something about words, and even syntax, in the first year of life' (2010, p. 5).

So when does a baby first encounter language? A baby is exposed to sound before conception as they hear sounds through the womb wall – sounds of everyday life.

For example, newborns seem to recognise familiar environmental sounds and melodies from the prenatal environment, discriminate between the native language of the mother and other languages, and distinguish the mother's voice from voices of other females. It has been suggested that prenatal learning facilitates, for example, language learning in infancy and provides a basis for attachment (Partanen et al., 2013).

There has been research that has started a 'trend' for exposing the baby in the womb to such sounds as classical music in an attempt to promote a child's future achievements. Whether this is valid is still debated; however, knowledge of the sounds presented to a baby in the womb can be very useful.

Case study

When first baby sitting, a grandmother is not yet fully aware of her grandchild's personal communication, unlike the mother, so when faced with a crying baby at 10 at night she reverts to her daughter's comment that Oliver likes the music from *Glee*! The grandmother is sceptical but in desperation she decides to give it a go and to her surprise the baby is instantly calmed. The grandmother now knows what her daughter was listening to in those months, weeks and days before Oliver was born.

Yes, this could be anecdotal and pure coincidence but it is something worth considering when caring for young children. As a practitioner ask yourself how many times you have asked parents during the admission process if there is any music that a baby has shown a preference for? I should imagine that the answer to this would be never, and yet think how useful that piece of information could be when a baby is distressed. When Saxton (2010) discusses this he goes further to say that, 'Even more remarkable, the unborn baby can learn to recognise the telling of a particular story' (p. 5). This does not mean to say that babies can understand and comprehend the story but rather that they are firstly tuned in to their mother's voice, but more importantly that it is the intonation, the rhythmic rise and fall of the voice that is the key. It is this musicality of the voice which helps babies to tune into language.

We all know that when we hear someone talk to a baby there is a change, a softness in the tone and that there is more of an emphasis on the rise and fall of the intonation – a sing-song type of speech. Women appear to do this naturally, and not just mothers. This interaction of the adult develops further as children begin to respond

(Continued)

(Continued)

to the sing-song voices that are often adopted when talking to babies – frequently called 'motherese'. The baby again responds to the rise and fall of the voice enjoying the sounds of words. Trevarthen and Malloch (2000) report research where mothers have sung nursery rhymes repeated over and over again to their babies. When the recordings are analysed it can be seen that as time progresses the baby is ahead of the mother; is in fact leading the singing of the song. This can be developed to the singing of songs and action rhymes, along with the reading and sharing of books which explore the complexity of language through alliteration and onomatopoeia, the first aspect of Phase One of *Letters and Sounds* (DfES, 2007). This early interaction is the introduction of phonics teaching.

Activity

Record an adult having a conversation with children at different ages (six months, one year, 18 months and so on until five years old) and see if you can notice the differences that the adult uses in their conversation when talking to another adult or to the children at different ages. What happens to the intonation? Are there any differences in body language or gesture? Is there any difference in the speed of the language used?

As with all learning and development in the early years we have to be wary of applying a 'one size fits all' development process. All babies will differ in the time they produce their first words, as all babies differ for when they take their first step. All babies are unique in their individual development process. An example would be three siblings who each reach their developmental milestones at different ages and not necessarily in the same order. However, a baby generally speaks their first word at around the age of one year with, usually for the parents, the memorable saying of either mama or dada (or various versions of these words); these sounds are repetitious and are part of a baby's babbling to which we as adults begin to attach meaning. We are giving the sound a name for an object; in this case the mother or father. As Saxton states, 'All in all, words and their meanings seem to present the child with a massively daunting learning problem'

(2010, p. 10). How is the baby to know that 'mother' is the name for a particular person in their life; does this word apply to all women or just women with blonde hair? How does the baby unravel the complexities of deciphering what word applies to which specific object/person? Does this come when the baby hears the string of other words that accompany this naming word, for instance 'your mother', 'Oliver's mother', etc.?

As children learn words and use single utterances they then need to exemplify this so that by adding words they can make their meaning clearer, and as they begin to use more words in strings then they have to use them in the right order: sentences, syntax.

Looking at the National Strategies can be of use to develop an understanding of general language and communication development in the earliest years (Table 2.1).

In order to meet the needs of babies, toddlers and young children it is important to have an understanding of how children develop in the very earliest stages. This is more than being familiar with the EYFS (DfE, 2012b), *Development Matters* statements (Early Education, 2012) or *Early Years Outcomes* (DfE, 2013b), which are only meant to give a broad understanding of where children should be and what progress they should be making. If there was to be a book to describe all of the different stages, you would probably need a library to store it in and an annexe to keep updating it whenever a new piece of research was introduced.

With this importance in mind let's discuss how we can meet this challenge when it comes to communication. *Every Child a Talker* (DCSF, 2008b) shows us that babies develop their language through having good role models; this does not mean that adults have to constantly talk to and question children, but rather that they should listen to the babbling of babies as if it were a conversation, which it is. Leave pauses so the young child knows that you are listening to them thus giving them the model for turn taking – a conversation. In an experiment called the 'still face' (Murray and Andrews, 2000) researchers demonstrate how the close interaction of adults can have an impact on the young baby. In this experiment the mother is making strong eye contact with her baby, talking and listening to him, using facial expression and being animated, which the baby responds to by making rapid arm and leg movements, showing real excitement. This continues until a signal from the researcher tells the mother to present a still and impassive face to her baby. The reaction is dramatic as within seconds the baby begins to show signs of distress, becomes disinterested and disengaged, and generally displays the body language of impassiveness. To see a similar experiment in action go to www.youtube.com/watch?v= apzXGEbZht0 or search for 'still face experiment'.

Table 2.1 Early Communication and Language

Stage	Listening and attention	Understanding (receptive language)	Talking (expressive language)	Social communication
0–11 months	Turns toward a familiar sound then locates a range of sounds with accuracy. Listens to, distinguishes and responds to intonations and sounds of voices. Quietens or alerts to the sound of speech. Fleeting attention – not under child's control, new stimulus takes whole attention.	Stops and looks when hears own name. **(by 12 months ⊠)**	Gradually develops speech sounds (babbling) to communicate with adults; says sounds like *baba, nono, gogo*. **(by 11 months ⊠)**	Gazes at faces and copies facial movements, e.g. sticking out tongue. Concentrates intently on faces and enjoys interaction. Uses voice, gesture, eye contact and facial expression to make contact with people and keep their attention. **(by 12 months ⊠)**
8–20 months	Concentrates intently on an object or activity of own choosing for short periods. Pays attention to dominant stimulus – easily distracted by noises or other people talking. Moves whole body to sounds they enjoy, such as music or a regular beat. Has a strong exploratory impulse.	Responds to the different things said when in a familiar context with a special person (e.g. *Where's Mummy?, Where's your nose?*). Understanding of single words in context is developing, e.g. '*cup*', '*milk*', '*daddy*'.	Uses single words. **(by 16 months ⊠)** Frequently imitates words and sounds. Enjoys babbling and increasingly experiments with using sounds and words to communicate for a range of purposes (e.g. teddy, more, no, bye-bye).	Likes being with familiar adult and watching them. Developing the ability to follow an adult's body language, including pointing and gesture. Learns that their voice and actions have effects on others. Uses pointing with eye gaze to make requests, and to share an interest. **(by 18 months ⊠)**
16–26 months	Listens to and enjoys rhythmic patterns in rhymes and stories. Enjoys rhymes and demonstrates listening by	Selects familiar objects by name and will go and find objects when asked, or identify objects from a group.	Beginning to put two words together (e.g. *want ball, more juice*). **(by 24 months ⊠)** Uses different types of everyday words (nouns, verbs and	Gradually able to engage in 'pretend' play with toys (supports child to imagine another's point of view).

Stage	Listening and attention	Understanding (receptive language)	Talking (expressive language)	Social communication
	trying to join in with actions or vocalisations. Rigid attention – may appear not to hear.		adjectives, e.g. *banana, go, sleep, hot*). Beginning to ask simple questions.	Looks to others for responses which confirm, contribute to or challenge their understanding.
22–36 months	Single-channelled attention. Can shift to a different task if attention fully obtained – using child's name helps focus. **(by 36 months ⊠)** Listens with interest to the noises adults make when they read stories. Recognises and responds to many familiar sounds, e.g. turning to a knock on the door, looking at or going to the door.	Identifies action words by pointing to the right picture, e.g. *Who's jumping?* **(by 30 months ⊠)** Understands 'who', 'what', 'where' in simple questions (e.g. *Who's that/can?, What's that?, Where is?*). Developing understanding of simple concepts (e.g. *big/little*).	Learns new words very rapidly and is able to use them in communicating. Uses action, sometimes with limited talk, that is largely concerned with the 'here and now' (e.g. reaches toward toy, saying *I have it*). Uses a variety of questions (e.g. *what, where, who*). Uses simple sentences (e.g. *Mummy gonna work*). Beginning to use word endings (e.g. *going, cats*).	Uses language as a powerful means of widening contacts, sharing feelings, experiences and thoughts. Holds a conversation, jumping from topic to topic. Enjoys being with and talking to adults and other children. Interested in others' play and will join in. Responds to the feelings of others.
30–50 months	Listens to others one to one or in small groups, when conversation interests them. Listens to stories with increasing attention and recall. Joins in with repeated refrains and anticipates key events and phrases in rhymes and stories. Focusing attention – still listen **or** do, but can shift own attention.	Understands use of objects (e.g. *What do we use to cut things?*). Shows understanding of prepositions such as 'under', 'on top', 'behind' by carrying out an action or selecting correct picture. Beginning to understand 'why' and 'how' questions.	Beginning to use more complex sentences to link thoughts (e.g. using *and, because*). Can retell a simple past event in correct order (e.g. *went down slide, hurt finger*). Uses talk to connect ideas, explain what is happening and anticipate what might happen next, recall and relive past experiences.	Beginning to accept the needs of others, with support. Can initiate conversations. Shows confidence in linking up with others for support and guidance. Talks freely about their home and community. Forms friendships with other children.

(Continued)

Table 2.1 (Continued)

Stage	Listening and attention	Understanding (receptive language)	Talking (expressive language)	Social communication
	Is able to follow directions (if not intently focused on own choice of activity).		Questions why things happen and gives explanations (e.g. asks *who, what, when, how*). Uses a range of tenses (e.g. *play, playing, will play, played*).	
40–60+ months	Sustains attentive listening, responding to what they have heard with relevant comments, questions or actions. Maintains attention, concentrates and sits quietly when appropriate. Two-channelled attention – can listen and do for short span. Integrated attention – can listen and do in range of situations with range of people; varies according to the demands of the task.	Understands humour (e.g. nonsense rhymes, jokes). Demonstrates understanding of 'how?' and 'why?' questions by giving explanations. Able to follow a story without pictures or props. Understands instructions containing sequencing words: first … after … last, and more abstract concepts: long, short, tall, hard, soft, rough.	Extends vocabulary, especially by grouping and naming, exploring the meaning and sounds of new words. Links statements and sticks to a main theme or intention. Uses language to imagine and recreate roles and experiences in play situations. Uses talk to organise, sequence and clarify thinking, ideas, feelings and events. Introduces a storyline or narrative into their play.	Has confidence to speak to others about their own wants, interests and opinions. Initiates conversation, attends to and takes account of what others say. Explains own knowledge and understanding, and asks appropriate questions of others. Shows awareness of the listener when speaking. Expresses needs/feelings in appropriate ways. Forms good relationships with adults and peers. Works as part of a group or class, taking turns.

Source: The National Strategies

Notes on monitoring early communication and language

Observation and best-fit judgements

- Judgements of a child's stage of development are made through a process of ongoing observational assessment.
- Observation involves noticing what children do and say in a range of contexts, and includes information from the family about what children do and say at home.
- For children learning English as an additional language, it is important to find out from families about how children use language in their mother tongue and how they communicate at home.
- The assessment is a 'best fit' match to a stage band. This involves considering what is known about the child, and matching it to the development described in the bands. This should be considered separately for each strand of communication and language.
- Within each band, a judgement will be made in two levels – either 'Emerging' when a child shows some development at that level, or 'Secure' when most of the statements reflect the child's current development.
- Development of speech sounds need not be assessed specifically, but it is useful to be aware of typical development which is described in the table to the right.

Checkpoints

- Alongside the 'best fit' judgement, certain 'Checkpoint' statements are included. Marked with a flag ⚑ and a specific age, these are particular statements which should be noted.
- Where a child has not reached a Checkpoint by the age indicated, this is not necessarily a sign of difficulty. The Checkpoint statements serve as an alert for close monitoring including discussion with the family, and perhaps further assessment or support.

Guidance on typical development of speech sounds

Stage	Speech sounds
	(Developing speech and being understood applies to all languages. Order of acquiring specific sounds – hare in English – may vary with other languages.)
0–11 months	Babbles using a range of sound combinations, with changes in pitch, rhythm and loudness.
	Babbles with intonation and rhythm of home language 'jargon'.
8–20 months	Speech consists of a combination of 'jargon' and some real words and may be difficult to understand.
16–26 months	Many immature speech patterns, so speech may not be clear.
	May leave out last sounds or substitute sounds (e.g. 'tap' for 'cap').
	Uses most vowels, and *m, p, b, n, t, d, w, h.*
22–36 months	Speech becoming clearer, and usually understood by others by 36 months although some immature speech patterns still evident.
	May still substitute sounds or leave out last sound. Emerging sounds including *k, g, f, s, z, i, y.*
30–50 months	Speech mostly can be understood by others even in connected speech.
	Emerging use of *ng, sh, ch, j, v, th, r* – may be inconsistent. Sound clusters emerging (e.g. *pl* in *play, sm* in *smile*) though some may be simplified (e.g. *gween* for *green*).
40–60+ months	Overall fully intelligible to others.
	May be still developing *r* and *th.*
	May simplify complex clusters (e.g. *skr, str*).

Making good progress

- The goal of monitoring children's development is to plan and provide more accurate support for each child to make good progress.
- How well a setting helps children to make good progress can be determined by analysing the proportion of children who are at risk of delay, as expected, or ahead of expectations in each strand of language and communication. If children are making accelerated progress, the proportion of children at risk of delay should decrease over time.
- In considering whether a child is at risk of delay, as expected, or ahead in each strand of language and communication, it is necessary to consider the child's actual age in months in relation to the overlapping age bands. If a child is within two months of the end of the age band and development is not yet within the band or is judged to be 'Emerging', then a judgement of 'risk of delay' would be appropriate.

As children grow older, adults need to be very conscious of how they interact with them; they should avoid questioning, which is meaningless when the adult already knows the answer. Rather we should be asking open-ended questions which encourage children to think and speculate. We need to leave a 'listening space' so that they have thinking time, time to order thoughts and time to respond. We need to be aware of the noise that constantly surrounds us. We as adults get weary of background noise that makes listening so difficult – how much more difficult for a child who has yet to develop the skills of filtering the noise of modern society? Music should be used intentionally to encourage young minds to listen and respond, not as a 'filler' and because everyone expects nursery rhymes to be on. We will expand on the concept of a good 'listening space' in subsequent chapters.

In our talk with babies and young children we often need to model language so that if a young child comes up holding a car and then says the word 'car', we respond by giving the model of word-strings to make sentences, 'Yes it's a red car'. Thus demonstrating how to put words together as well as making links with the child's thoughts and actions.

Communication within the first few months of life is largely with those people who are close to the baby, especially the parents. It is important to remember that one of the first things that has to be in place for a baby to develop is for them to feel safe and secure in their early relationships. It is this attachment from birth which helps to establish the right conditions for learning to take place.

Before we move on to look at the early interactions of babies and adults it is important for us to consider attachment and emotional well-being so that the right conditions for babies to interact are established. It is a natural phenomenon for babies to attach strongly to their mothers, but this does not always happen (Leach, 2010), and for many reasons, such as separation at birth or for periods of time due to illness, there may be a disruption in this attachment or the attachment may be formed with someone other than the mother. If we are going to look at attachment then we have to refer to the work of Bowlby. Bowlby (1989, p. 8) described the importance of attachment as, 'the vital importance of a stable and permanent relationship with a loving mother (or mother substitute) throughout infancy and childhood'. Much of Bolwby's research about attachment has come under criticism (Rutter, 1972; Fonagy, 2001), especially when discussing the role of the mother as the primary carer. Challenges to Bowlby's theory assert that babies can form multiple attachments and that in some cases being in the sole care of the mother can have detrimental effects for the baby (Rutter, 1972). Although Bowlby's work was manipulated by the government (in order to encourage or even force women from the workforce at the end of the Second World War and ensure employment for returning soldiers), his theory still resonates today when so many of our youngest children are attending out-of-home day care settings. In keeping with the now more commonly held belief that babies and young children can form multiple attachments it is important that we recognise how establishing a close relationship can impact on development. As Stern writes,

> so much of attachment consists of the memories and mental models of what happens between you and that other person: How you feel about them. What they can make you experience that others cannot. (Stern, 1991, p. 7)

The work of Ferre Laevers (1994) on experiential learning gives a framework for assessing babies' and young children's well-being. This assessment tool is in line with the concept of rigorous assessment as a necessary tool as highlighted by Rose (2006). If the well-being scales are applied when observing young children we can make a calculated assessment of what their well-being is like during an interaction. If we refer back to the still face experiment (Murray and Andrews, 2000) described earlier, we can see how there are high levels of well-being when there is involvement on the part of both the mother and the baby. The baby's emotional well-being is high when the mother is interacting and maintaining good eye contact; this would be evidenced by the relaxed positioning of the body, and the excited and rapid movements of the limbs in anticipation. If, however, we were to assess the well-being when the mother stops the interaction and loses eye contact then the baby's well-being would be low; this would be evidenced by the change in the body language as the baby becomes distressed and starts to become unable to manage their emotions. What we also see is that as the baby's level of well-being drops so does their ability to remain involved at a high level. Well-being and involvement are inextricably linked; in order to be involved a baby/child needs to have high levels of well-being. Laevers (1994) describes this as follows:

- Children with a high level of well-being feel great. They enjoy life to the full
- They have fun, take joy in each other and in their surroundings
- They radiate vitality as well as relaxation and inner peace
- They adopt an open and receptive attitude towards their environment
- They are spontaneous and can fully be themselves
- Well-being is linked to self-confidence, a good degree of self-esteem and resilience
- All this is based on being in touch with themselves, with their own feelings and experiences, fresh and pure

Therefore, if we want babies and young children to be challenged and to learn then we have to support and look after their well-being in order to involve them in this process.

Babies at home

Before we consider the importance of communication and interaction within day care settings we first have to consider what needs to happen in the home. The majority of babies enter day care or out-of-home provision at approximately nine months of age to one year. This means that babies have already had opportunities to begin their language development. It is important therefore that on our journey of communication and interaction that we begin with what has happened in the home and the baby's role within a nuclear family unit.

What can families, and more importantly parents do to help with the development of their baby's communication skills? As a starting point we have to assume that a baby has high levels of emotional well-being and that in most cases strong attachments have been formed. One of the phrases used by Roberts (2010) in her book, *Wellbeing from Birth*, is *Companionable Apprenticeship*. Roberts describes this in relation to children's well-being, but as we have already discussed, a baby's development is inextricably linked to their emotional well-being. Roberts (2010) describes this phrase as about being together and sharing in the lives of the family community and recognises that, 'Children's routine involvement in real-life tasks is a wonderfully rich context for *all* the wellbeing constructs' (p. 65). This obviously links very closely to baby's initial communication exposure.

So how can parents develop this apprenticeship with their babies? One of the major difficulties that is encountered in our modern digital society is the way digital technology interferes with the development of this apprenticeship relationship. Take for example a mother pushing a pram with her iPod or mobile phone to her ear (Clare, 2012, p. 30). This digital interaction is not doing the communication skills or development of our very youngest children any favours; as these tools become more and more a part of our everyday lives we frequently lose sight of how much time we as adults devote to their use. In a conversation with another adult recently when discussing the use of digital technology she said that she was amazed when reading a magazine that she had started to try and scroll the page before realising that the magazine was not a touch screen! Or how common is it now that when you sit down with a group of people you notice that some of the group are interacting with their phones rather than with another person? If parents become absorbed in this interaction they are not giving their child the oppor-tunity to develop the links in their brain to see the importance of a two-way interaction – conversation.

As part of a baby's apprenticeship, mothers (for it is in fact mothers who in most cases are the primary carers for babies when they are very young) should be very aware of the importance of making eye contact with their baby and engaging them in 'conversation' by modelling language and its usage. Just as day care providers, as we shall discuss later, need to ensure that there are good listening spaces in the setting, then so too should par-ents by keeping the background noise to a minimum when talking with a baby. As Saxton (2010, p. 86) notes, the children of talkative mothers develop larger vocabularies simply from the extent of exposure to lan-guage. Additionally, as Snow (1997, p. 21) argues, it is the way that mothers talk to their babies, with the belief that the babies are capable of reciprocal communication that also leads to this development.

In a home, unlike in day care, babies can experience a wealth of words by being exposed to a vocabulary that is 'home orientated' – the language of hanging the washing on the line, the language of folding clothes, of preparing food and perhaps one of the most important for me, the lan-guage of the community environment. Consider all those noises that are present in everyday life in the outdoors: birds singing, cars moving, trees blowing. If attention is bought to these then babies will make the con-nections in their brains to listening to, to tuning in to other sounds (potentially the beginning of an awareness of phonics). I conducted some research (unpublished) looking at the ways in which mothers develop a relationship with their babies. This was done through structured conver-sations with mothers asking them about their relationships with their babies from birth to six months. One of the questions asked in these discussions was around *Companionable Apprenticeship*, asking how their baby was a part of their everyday real life experiences. One mother clearly demonstrates how parents can be involved in this language apprenticeship with their baby:

> I tell him what I am doing. We have a chat. When doing the washing we talk about the trees because he loves them and when I am dusting he follows me around.

Another opportunity for babies and parents to interact occurs when going out shopping or for walks with a buggy. As discussed in Clare (2012) research has demonstrated that prams that are forward-facing restrict the number of opportunities for parents and babies to interact (www.talktoy-ourbaby.com). The research was further enhanced by a video (http://

vimeo.com/10581078) which highlighted what the world looks like from the perspective of a baby or young child in a forward-facing pram by placing a camera in the buggy. This research has been developed in New Zealand where researchers found that

> While communication may be easier when using a parent-facing pram, parents can still have valuable language interactions with children when using forward-facing prams. Occasionally pausing to bend down to make face-to-face contact with the child can extend on the benefits of these interactions. (Blaiklock, 2013, p. 26)

The case study which follows shows how a baby and his mother engage in *Companionable Apprenticeship* as he is being dressed in the morning.

Case study

Oscar aged five months

At the start of the observation the mother tells me that she tries to make good eye contact with her son, at the same time as being tactile with him by blowing raspberries on his tummy – just talking to him because he doesn't like getting dressed. She explains that she does this before she tries to dress him, as well as at the end of the routine; this interaction reassures him and calms him down.

During the routine of dressing him the mother maintains a closeness with Oscar through eye contact, physical contact and verbal interaction. As she puts his clothes on she involves him in the process; as each article of clothing is put on she offers him choices such as plain or stripey T-shirt, showing them to him as well as verbally describing and naming them. She also links this activity to his wider social context by telling him he is dressing like his daddy and that the T-shirt was one that his auntie Hannah bought him

So what does this case study reveal? This is a mother who is well aware of the need for her son to have high levels of emotional well-being (Laevers, 1994) before she can involve him in the disliked dressing routine. She is engaging with Roberts' (2010) concept of *Companionable Apprenticeship* as she talks about the clothes he has 'chosen'. She demonstrates her key knowledge of her son which has come about as a result of a strong attachment (Bowlby, 1989) and his position in his family community, which has echoes of Bronfenbrenner's ecological model (1979), which leaves the child at the centre being affected by the near and distant communities that are an influence on his life. It is clear in this short interaction that the mother's interaction with her child has had an impact on him and that her stimulation has evoked a positive response. As Stern (1991, p. 67) states, 'The more stimulation a baby is exposed to, the more he will be activated or excited. This direct relationship between the intensity of stimulation from the outside (performed by the mother) and that of the excitation evoked in the baby is a general rule for mother–infant interactions.'

Activity

Conduct an observation (written or video) of an adult interacting with a baby. Use Table 2.2 to analyse the observation.

Table 2.2   Observation analysis

Concepts	Date: Context:
Companiable Attention (Roberts, 2010)	How does your baby know that they have your full attention? (Prompts: body language, eye contact, verbal language)
Companiable Apprenticeship (Roberts, 2010)	How is your baby part of everyday/real life experiences? (Prompts: joining in, commentary on everyday experiences)
Well-being (Laevers, 1994)	How does the adult ensure high levels of well-being?
Attachment (Bowlby, 1989)	How does the adult demonstrate an attachment with the child?
Community (Bronfenbrenner, 1979)	How does the adult make links with baby's community (family, experiences)?

Another way in which parents can contribute to their child's communication and literacy development is through sharing stories. The earlier that babies are exposed to alternative methods of communication such as the written word the better. Many people believe that sharing stories with very young babies is meaningless, but this is about making connections as well as developing the bond between parents and their baby. In their research Farrant and Zubrick (2012, p. 346) found that, 'parent–child book reading provides an excellent opportunity for vocabulary expansion by learning word–object mappings in a more structured setting'.

If parents share books with babies they can further develop the emotional bond or attachment, as this can be a very special 'close time' when parent and baby can 'snuggle' in and share. No matter how young a baby, the sharing of books is important because as Schickedanz (1999, p. 11) explains, 'even very young babies like books and engage with them in rather remarkable ways'.

For many mothers today there are opportunities to take their babies to organised language events which are often arranged by their local Children's Centre. These events can range from story times in the local library or in independent bookshops (I know one where the proprietors have story times for different age groups), to Rhymetimes events, to the sharing of information about good practice from organisations such as the National Literacy Trust (www.wordsforlife.org.uk/).

Questions for reflection

Consider how you engage with parents when they first attend your setting; do you ask them about the things that they have done with their children, for instance reading books?

How could you further develop the concept of *Companionable Apprenticeship* in your setting?

Further reading

- Stern, D (1991). *Diary of a Baby*. New York: Basic Books.

In this book Stern draws on his background in psychiatry to present a re-creation of a baby's world. He discusses what a baby is thinking and feeling in a thought-provoking manner. This book can be read alongside Stern's *The Birth of a Mother* (1998), where he discusses the concept of being 'good enough'.

- Schickedanz, J (1999). *Much More than the ABC's*. Washington: National Association for the Education of Young Children.

This book looks at how babies and young children develop their literacy skills before entering school. It is grounded in research and offers suggestions as to how parents, carers and practitioners can support this development.

3

Interaction and communication of babies and toddlers

This chapter will:

- Discuss the importance of the key person in interactions
- Look at the typical language development in babies between the ages of one and two years
- Examine the link between the area of Communication and Language and the role of the practitioners
- Introduce a table for observing adult interactions

Before commencing our discussion about communication and interaction in a baby room it is pertinent to state what I believe a baby room to be. For the purposes of this chapter a baby room will be the room (or in some nurseries, rooms) that accommodate babies from birth to two years old. Most babies are between nine months and one year when they first access this room but there are babies who start much earlier. In this room in the UK the ratio of adults to children is 1:3, which means that there is the potential for high levels of close interaction.

Emotional well-being and the key person

When a baby first begins to attend a day care setting the most important factor in their development is that their well-being is high. As has already been stated, if children have low levels of well-being then this has an impact on their progress in all areas of cognitive development (see Chapter 2). This is why when a baby goes to an out-of-home care setting it is important that there is a good settling-in process which involves both the baby and the parents. As part of this settling-in process the parents and the child should be developing a close relationship with the child's key worker. As part of this relationship development the practitioner needs to ensure that they use the knowledge that the parents have about their child to begin to form their relationship and to establish close links between home and setting.

When we gather information from parents we are usually very good at finding out all of the vital administrative information, but as I (Clare, 2012, p. 22) demonstrate in the model I developed using some of the criteria gained from studying Bronfenbrenner's (1979) ecological model, there is more information that could be gathered which would give a better understanding of the child and their family. In the gathering of this information we rarely ask parents about their child's cognitive development. If we are being honest, when a baby registers for care within a setting the questions tend to be centred on their routines and their physical needs. Would a setting ever consider asking parents how their baby communicates with them?

Activity

In your setting, have a meeting with the baby room practitioners and discuss the ways in which the babies in their room interact, and consider how you support this communication and interaction.

- Do they babble?
- Do they turn take in conversation?
- Do they respond to certain adults because of their tone of voice?
- Are they more responsive when there is music playing?
- Do you know what a baby's favourite book is?

In order for this relationship to become embedded within practice it is important that the key person spends quality time with their key children and this can only be achieved if the staffing in the room enables this to occur. Although there has been much recent debate (*Guardian*, 2013) about staffing ratios for children in nurseries (DfE, 2013a), in 2013 the government retained historical ratios of 1:3 for babies and under twos and 1:4 for children aged between two and three, instead of proposed ratios of 1:4 for children under two and 1:6 for children aged two to three.

If these ratios had changed, then practitioners in a room would have been busier, caring for more children, and their relationships would be less strong and the interactions weakened. I always have this vision of going into a baby room where all the babies are crying (one baby crying usually has a knock-on effect) and the adult, with a ratio of 1:3 is trying to calm three babies by cradling two in her arms with the third being rocked in a cradle by the adult's foot; my reaction is that it would be physically impossible to then add a fourth baby to this scene, let alone meet the emotional needs of any if not all of the babies.

Language development: 12 months to two years

Babies are usually aged about nine months to one year old when they first enter a day nursery and therefore have already had a considerable period of time in which to develop their early language skills within their home environment (see Chapter 2). Considering that children learn implicitly, there is much that they can or will have learnt by the time that they arrive at a setting. In a communication context, 'by 18 months of age, 75% of typically developing children understand about 150 words and can successfully produce 50 words' (Kuhl, 2004, p. 834). We can see that children progress in language in a relatively short period of time.

Although nurseries are often registered to take babies from birth, most typically babies are aged from about 12 months to two years of age. As the ECAT monitoring tool (see Chapter 2) shows us, this is a stage when children need to be in close proximity to adults; it is only when the adult is close that a baby can interact through facial expression. As we have seen in the still face experiment (Murray and Andrews, 2000) babies love to look at faces; it seems that they are pre-programmed to do this, 'they appear to come into the world "programmed" to have preferences for human faces and human beings and movements' (David et al., 2003, p. 13).

Between the ages of nine months and 24 months a baby's language is still unclear, especially for those who are unfamiliar with the baby. It is amazing when we eavesdrop on 'conversations' between mothers and their babies, that mothers appear to be fully aware of what their baby is trying to say, whilst to us, as strangers, it is as difficult to understand as a foreign language. This ability to 'tune in' to a baby's communication is further evidence which stresses the importance of practitioners in day care settings establishing close and familiar relationships with their key babies.

Before defining what language at this age is like it would seem appropriate to look at and define the different aspects (and terminology) of language development.

- Grammar (syntax): Is how a language uses rules to define how words are put together to make sentences – the order in which words need to go in order for them to make sense to the listener (and reader)
- Morphology: Is the separate parts of words such that *good* is one morpheme and can stand on its own as a word whereas *goodness* is two morphemes (*good* + *ness*) and so on
- Phonology: Is the system of sounds in a language, and the speech sounds in words are known as phonemes

As a baby is developing language all the above aspects are acquired as they listen to the way in which words and sentences are put together. It is no use a child acquiring a large vocabulary of single words if they do not acquire the ability to put these words together so that there is an agreed understanding of what is being said, they would be developing language but not the skills to communicate.

When a baby typically first starts at a day nursery they have spent a long time listening and as they begin to say their first words they are ready to make progress using all that they have heard. As adults we speak at a fast rate, so for the baby to be able to distinguish between the different sounds or phonemes is a daunting task. As adults we naturally slow the pace of our speech when talking to young children, just as we do when talking to people who do not speak our language. It is quite common for babies and young children to focus on the words at the beginning and end of sentences, therefore we need to keep our sentences simple so that the baby can tune into the key messages of what is being said. This does not mean that we use over-simplified language with children but rather that we are aware of the complexities of our language and make allowances for the learner.

When babies first start to use words, their vocabulary focuses around those things and people who are of interest to them. No matter what families or socio-economic background children come from, their worlds revolve around common activities and interests in which they are involved. For example, words associated with food, body parts, family, animals, actions and favourite toys/objects (Saxton, 2010).

When they start to vocalise words babies often make 'mistakes' according to the complexity of the sound they are trying to say. For example, my grandson would indicate that he wanted you to sit on the 'bloor' (floor) to play with him. He could say 'mama' and 'dada' but his name for me, as the following case study demonstrates, became a family anecdote.

Case study

When Oscar began to utter his first words I was perturbed (and I admit a little upset) that the one name that he couldn't (or possibly wouldn't say) was Grannie. I had chosen my name because I could then be known as Grannie Annie, thus introducing some rhyming to my very young grandson. However, I used to talk to him over-pronouncing my title with an exaggerated 'Gr' sound followed by the '...annie'. I thought this would be difficult because I knew two consonant sounds together was a hard task for such a young child. What did surprise me, and made us all laugh was that he started to make a 'Grrrrrrrrrrrr' sound whenever he saw me but showed no signs of being able to join the two sounds together to give me my title. I to this day am still referred to as 'Grrrr'!!

The role of the practitioner within interaction

So what can the practitioner in the baby room do to encourage, challenge and extend the communication/vocabulary of our very youngest talkers? For me the experiences that we offer in the baby room are the primary drivers of helping children to develop their communication skills. These experiences *do not* have to be contrived activities that we think we *should* be doing, but rather everyday occurrences which stimulate the senses and which are accompanied by rich and appropriate interactions that give babies and young children the opportunity to hear vocabulary used in context which is linked to experiences, feelings (sensory and emotional) and objects.

As with all development it is social interaction which has an influence on children's learning. Human beings are intrinsically social and it is through this that children's communication develops. As Kuhl (2004, p. 836) states, 'social deprivation, whether imposed by humans or caused by atypical brain function, has a devastating effect on language acquisition'.

An activity in a baby room is illustrated in the following case study which involves a baby and adult engaged in tummy time, which is an activity which plays an important part in a baby's physical development.

Tummy time is an important activity because it strengthens the baby's upper body and neck muscles and also gives them the opportunity to get a peripheral view of the world. See the poster from the Association of Paediatric Chartered Physiotherapists explaining more about tummy time, available at http://apcp.csp.org.uk/publications/tummy-time-poster.

Case study

On entering the baby room I notice a practitioner lying on her tummy on the floor. In front of her is a baby, also lying on her tummy. The aim of this activity is to encourage the baby, who does not like to lie on her tummy, to stay in this position for as long as possible to gain benefit from the activity. But this wasn't just about promoting this baby's physical development; the pair were facing one another and as the baby raised her head she made eye contact with the adult who then began to engage the little girl in conversation. The interaction, which lasted for over five minutes, was magical, as the baby's body language demonstrated that she was at ease with this adult and also because her facial expression showed that she was communicating; following the lead of the adult she was involved in a 'chilled out' interaction.

Let's look at some of the things that we may do in order to demonstrate that babies and young children are developing and making progress in line with the EYFS *Outcomes* (DfE, 2013b). Table 3.1 gives a summary of these outcomes, and those that are in bold are discussed explicitly within this chapter. This can act as a good prompt for communication, especially when used in conjunction with the assessment tool at the end of this chapter.

Table 3.1   Extracts from the EYFS *Outcomes* (DfE, 2013b) illustrating the discussions of the strands within the area of Communication and Language

Listening and attention	
8 to 20 months	**Moves whole bodies to sounds they enjoy, such as music or a regular beat.**
Typically the age when babies begin to attend out-of-home day care settings.	Has a strong exploratory impulse.
Babies can stay in the same room until they are mobile or they can remain in a room which caters for children under the age of two.	Concentrates intently on an object or activity of own choosing for short periods.
	Pays attention to dominant stimulus – easily distracted by noises or other people talking.

16 to 26 months As with all aspects of child development this should be based on the individual child. Babies and children do not achieve the same milestones at the same time, therefore there will be aspects from this age range that children two years and under will be competent at.	**Listens to and enjoys rhythmic patterns in rhymes and stories.** **Enjoys rhymes and demonstrates listening by trying to join in with actions or vocalisations.** Rigid attention – may appear not to hear.

Understanding

8 to 20 months	**Developing the ability to follow others' body language, including pointing and gesture.** **Responds to the different things said when in a familiar context with a special person (e.g. 'Where's Mummy? Where's your nose?').** **Understanding of single words in context is developing (e.g. 'cup', 'milk', 'daddy').**
16 to 26 months	Selects familiar objects by name and will go and find objects when asked, or identify objects from a group. Understands simple sentences (e.g. 'Throw the ball'.)

Speaking

8 to 20 months	**Uses sounds in play, e.g. 'brrrm' for toy car.** Uses single words. Frequently imitates words and sounds.
16 to 26 months When it comes to speaking you will notice that the outcomes are much less age-specific related.	Enjoys babbling and increasingly experiments with using sounds and words to communicate for a range of purposes (e.g. 'teddy', 'more', 'no', 'bye-bye'). **Uses pointing with eye gaze to make requests, and to share an interest.** **Creates personal words as they begin to develop language.**

Listening and attention

As has been discussed in the first chapter, all children enjoy rhythm and rhyme. When choosing books adults need to pay close attention to the language/vocabulary that is used and the way in which the words are used to create a rhythm. The following classic books are just a few examples of how rhyme and rhythm are used in books:

- *Where's my Teddy* – Jez Alborough
- *We're Going on a Bear Hunt* – Michael Rosen and Helen Oxenbury
- *Each Peach Pear Plum* – Janet and Allen Ahlberg
- *Peepo* – Janet and Allen Ahlberg
- *Round and Round the Garden* – Sarah Williams

- *The Very Hungry Caterpillar* – Eric Carle
- *Dear Zoo* – Rod Campbell

A useful web site to help practitioners and families select suitable books for babies and young children can be found at the Bookstart web site (www.bookstart.org.uk/), where there are book lists ordered by age appropriateness and category.

For me, there has to be increased attention paid to the inclusion of books in a setting, especially in the baby room, where tatty, poor quality board books or even worse grubby cloth books, are presented to our very youngest children with an attitude of 'these will do'! The importance of books should not be understated even for the youngest children.

Apart from books, children can enjoy rhyme and rhythm through singing and the introduction of action rhymes. However, singing is often used as a 'filler' because the children are sitting waiting for their lunches which are late. This can often mean children under two are expected to sit for long, large group sessions, where the length of the session and the size of the group is totally age inappropriate. I would rather see adults singing spontaneously with these young children within their play, linking it to what the child is doing or is interested in. Singing has to be done with a purpose, it has to be presented in an appropriate manner and it *has* to be quality if children are to develop their 'Listening and Attention' skills as highlighted in the EYFS *Outcomes* (DfE, 2013b) discussed below.

Another barrier to communication commonly occurring in day care settings is the use of background, nursery rhyme music. The use of music to give background noise is detrimental to babies' and young children's development of their listening skills. If there is too much background noise in a room then young children find it very difficult to listen to conversation. In the following short observation you can see how detrimental the use of music can be not only to the development of babies' listening skills but also to their emotional well-being.

Case study

I was conducting an Infant/Toddler Environmental Rating Scale (ITERS-R) (Harms et al., 2003) in a baby room at a large day nursery. When I entered the room at 8.45 to begin the audit, nursery rhymes were being played. This was not just background noise; it could be heard in the adjacent room. As I continued with the audit the music continued to play and as a consequence there was no interaction because no-one could hear anything other than the music. This continued until 10.30 when the music stopped; I was relieved. This, however, was short lived, the CD had just finished so the adult got up to put another CD on.

The only time during the three hours it took me to complete the audit that the music was not playing was when the babies were taken outside.

If I had also been looking at children's well-being I would have had to mark most of them as a low level 1's and 2's. There was an apathy about the body language of these babies. There was no talk and the children looked isolated and uninvolved.

Activity

In your setting consider the background noise; this may not be just music playing. This could be loud adults who are dominating the 'talking space', noise from other rooms and other external sounds, such as traffic. In discussion with your colleagues create some effective strategies to eliminate as much of the background noise as possible.

The following case study clearly illustrates how rhythm appeals to young children and how it can be used effectively to develop children's involvement and enjoyment.

Case study

In this observation Joe is 19 months old. He is a happy child who enjoys interacting and being with the adults in the room.

- Joe responds by smiling when he shakes the rattle close to his ear
- Ten minutes later at 9.25, Joe is still in the same position with the adult, just interacting with the toys that are within his reach

(Continued)

(Continued)

- He picks up the rain maker and tries to put it into a smaller box. He then starts to put other toys that will fit into the box
- He shakes the rattle and shows it to the adult beside him
- Joe is happy and smiles all the time but there is no vocalisation, especially as he has a dummy in his mouth
- Joe then becomes more vocal by making sounds as he laughs with the adult. He is really engaged with the adult
- The dummy is then removed and although Joe is still happy and he is laughing it is now 9.40 and he is still in the same position as at the beginning of the observation
- Joe then does stand up for a brief moment, makes eye contact with me and shakes the rattle. He then resumes his original position
- When I or the other adult make facial gestures Joe responds by laughing
- The adult beside him role models some language and Joe echoes it back to her
- The other adult in the room starts singing. Joe becomes more animated, he laughs and stands up to move rhythmically with the singing. He claps and laughs out loud. It is obvious that Joe really enjoys this activity as he becomes more involved – he continues to move and clap and also starts to do the actions to accompany the song
- When the singing stops Joe continues to move up and down
- Joe begins to make more noises – much louder – he is now more vocal and animated than at any other time during the observation. He begins to babble to himself but still stays in the same vicinity that he was in at the beginning of the observation until it is snack time
- When they start to sing 'Twinkle Twinkle' he points up for the star and he predicts the 'knock' on the door when they sing 'Miss Polly'. He also does all of the other actions
- Although he remains with the adult for this observation Joe is a very social child. This is evidenced by his happy disposition and the looks that he shares as if sharing a secret with the different adults that he makes eye contact with

Joe is not that verbal and the question that needs to be discussed is the use of a dummy. Although the practitioner sensitively took the dummy away, it was an ever-present object. Speech and language therapists will say that over-use of a comforter or dummy will have an

impact on the development of speech; often children who have continuous access to a dummy 'talk round' it, which makes their developing
speech even harder to understand. As Fox et al. (2002, p. 127) write
about their research into speech disorders, 'The speech-disordered
group was more likely than the control group to have used a dummy, a
bottle or a thumb as a pacifier for more than 24 months'.

Understanding

The people and objects that babies and young children encounter in their
first two years are named over and over again to reinforce the link between
the object and its name. As can be seen in the tool for observation introduced at the end of this chapter (Table 3.2), naming objects and narrating
what is happening are two kinds of interactions that the adult can use to
develop babies' knowledge of language and its use. To ensure that babies
and young children develop their understanding or comprehension of what
is spoken, adults need to provide experiences and activities that promote
understanding. By inference, this does involve a lot of naming and questioning, but it is imperative that the adult does not bombard the children
so that it feels as if they are being interrogated. The key to this is to make
everything fun and exciting and to use props to support the development
of understanding.

In the following case study you can see how the adult effectively
engages with the girl, and what follows is probably one of the best interactions between an adult and a baby that I have observed, especially looking
at the way in which the carer extended Maisie by asking her to recognise
the body parts 'outside' of herself.

Case study

Maisie is 18 months old and attends the setting five sessions a week.

- She is put in the bouncing chair as she does appear tired. The adult
  is next to her folding blankets and Maisie engages in a game of
  peek–a–boo with her. When this is finished she wants a cuddle from
  the adult and as she is lifted up she snuggles in. When she goes back

(Continued)

(Continued)

in the bouncer she makes good eye contact with the adult – she keeps looking over to me and smiling. When you ask her a question she responds

- Maisie is happy and smiling
- She starts to rock herself in the bouncer and she starts to wave her arms in time with the movements – this develops into strong bouncing, she is laughing and giggling as she does this. The adult then engages her with peek-a-boo behind her hands and encourages Maisie to cover/uncover her eyes so that they can play the game together – Maisie likes this
- The adult then starts a game of asking questions. What noise does the ...?
- And Maisie responds with the appropriate animal sound
- This develops into 'Where are your feet?' – Maisie responds correctly to all of this and so the adult develops this further by asking, 'Where are *my* feet?', and again Maisie responds
- Maisie now decides that she would like to get up
- Maisie says the names of the other children
- She goes over to pick up the balls and she babbles as she walks around with the balls

Maisie responded really well to this interaction.

Speaking

When it comes to the strand of speaking in relation to babies under two years of age, it is about the adult keying or tuning in to what the child wants to say. Frequently this entails looking at body language, gesture and expression in order to try and understand what is being said. Well-established relationships can also help with this translation or understanding.

We all know that very young children use the sounds from their environments in their earliest expressions of speech. As the EYFS *Outcomes* (DfE, 2013b) discuss, babies use sounds in their play. We see this when children are playing with toy cars ('brrrm') and emergency vehicles ('mema') as they deploy their emerging use of sounds to imitate the sounds that they hear. Not only do very young children use sounds in this way, they also use words which are made up. We have often contemplated what my grandson meant when he used the word 'DWAR'. At the time this word was important to him but none of his close family could decipher its meaning despite numerous attempts. This for young children is very frustrating; they have something important to say but as yet they do not have the skill to make themselves understood. In these situations adults have to be very patient and support children through these frustrations – help them to manage their feelings and try to seek alternative ways of communication. This could be to introduce the children to a system of signing, such as 'Signalong' as discussed in Chapter 1. Frequently children find this a very effective way of alleviating their frustrations but in order for this to be successful adults must be consistent in its use and it must, as with everything that is done with very young children, be continually repeated to ensure that children have a solid understanding. It must be used by all staff in a room and it must be reintroduced every time that a new child starts at the setting.

In the following case study we are introduced to a boy who relies on gesture and expression to communicate, in preference to vocalising.

Case study

James is 17 months old and has been attending the day nursery for some time. He is very attached to his blanket and his dummy and as a result rarely vocalises.

- James goes over to be by the adult and he plays a game of hide and seek with her using his blanket
- The adult ties his laces
- James uses hand gestures in response
- James steers the wheels as the adult sings car songs; he plays with the switches on the steering wheel – he twists and turns and presses
- James watches as the cars go down the slide with the adult and then he gets up
- James joins in with the singing of 'Wind the bobbin up', doing some of the actions
- He then joins in with the singing of 'One currant bun'. James claps and laughs through this

(Continued)

(Continued)

- The adult plays peek-a-boo again with James and his blanket
- James laughs during this game and then starts the game himself
- James uses a lot of facial expression during all of the interactions with the adults
- James sings more songs and becomes more animated – he does the actions and begins to make vocal noises – the first that he has really made all morning
- James engages in a game with the adult

James is always smiling, he is content and he enjoys looking at the adults in the room. James communicates through his facial expressions and gestures – he nods and holds his hands up but he rarely vocalises. Towards the end of this observation James screams with joy and the adult comments that this is a rare occurrence for him as he usually communicates by expression and gesture in preference to vocalising.

It is clear from this case study that the adult has engaged with James and has effectively used his comfort blanket to establish some interaction.

Tool for observation

Table 3.2 is a suggested tool for use when looking at the role of adult interaction. This tool is introduced here, but it is intended to be used for observing adult interactions with children of all ages within a nursery, and so also applies to the following chapters of this book. Observing adults is a useful tool for reflective practice and should have a place in any good quality day nursery. The observed interactions are listed on the left-hand side, with tick boxes on the right which are to be used when the type of interaction has occurred. This tool is not intended to be used to observe for a short period of time, but rather over a period of a session, or in a particular area, or during an activity or care routine. I would not expect during an observation to see all aspects of interaction used; what it might do is demonstrate to the practitioners that there are some areas of their interactions which need development. This tool could be used as part of an appraisal system within a nursery.

Table 3.2   Observing adult interactions

Date:											
Context:											
Observed interaction											
Making eye contact and being at their level											
Pulling faces											
Using gesture											
Making sounds											
Making up fun sounding words which do not always make sense but which enjoy the richness of the sounds that we can make											
Using intonation											
Repeating and echoing											
Narrating what is happening											
Singing, spontaneously as well as in groups											
Naming objects that are of interest to the baby											
Questioning with a purpose and which is meaningful											
Extending, not always using single words but building up to simple sentences (and as babies become older and more mobile, building sentences up with verbs and adjectives)											
Allowing space for silence											
Pausing											
Making links/connections to the objects and people who are important in a baby's life											
Using children's names/being personal											

Conclusion

This chapter has highlighted the role of the adult within interaction and established that the relationship between the practitioner (key person) and the baby or young child is central to achieving high levels of emotional well-being.

Further reading

- Jarman, E (2013) *The Communication Friendly Spaces Approach*. Ashford: Elizabeth Jarman Ltd.

This book demonstrates how the Communication Friendly Spaces (CFS™) Approach works. It is supported by case studies and has been used in a range of contexts to enable practitioners to make informed changes to their environments. This book will challenge you to consider how your environments support children's communication skills, emotional well-being and physical development. Also worth visiting is the web site: www.elizabeth jarmantraining.co.uk.

- Gopnik, A., Meltzoff, A. and Kuhl, P. (2001) *The Scientist in the Crib: What Early Learning Tells Us about the Mind*. New York: Harper.

This book looks into what we know about the brains of babies and young children. Of particular interest is Chapter 4, 'What Children Learn about Language'. In their preface the authors say, 'Part of the message of this book is that children can do so much because they have the help of people who care about them'.

4

Interaction and communication of children between two and three

This chapter will:

- Look at the typical language development in babies between the ages of two and three years
- Consider the way in which adult involvement in activities helps and supports toddlers' language and communication development
- Explore how adults can encourage early mark making

When discussing the toddler room I am referring to the room in a nursery where those children between the ages of two and three are cared for. There has been a recent growth in the number of two year olds accessing day care as part of the government's initiative of Early Intervention targeting children from lower socio-economic status (SES) homes. Research has shown that those children from higher SES homes have had more language input of a higher quality than children from low SES homes where, 'children from lower SES homes receive more prohibitions and fewer affirmations than children in higher SES homes' (Murray et al., 2006, p. 234). This low quality of input within their early stages in development has a knock-on effect on children's later language development: 'There appear to be clear advantages for children from low SES homes who attend high quality child care and experience a higher quantity and quality of language than in the home' (ibid., p. 238). Therefore it would seem appropriate for the government to intervene and try to secure quality childcare for children from low SES homes where the interactions may be of a higher quality.

This emphasis on quality has much relevance when we come to look at the interactions between toddlers and practitioners later in the chapter. One other question that arises is the adult-to-child ratio. If the targeting of two year olds for funding is about raising the quality of interactions then do we not also have to consider the amount of time that very busy practitioners are able to spend in 1:1 interaction? Interestingly, research has demonstrated that multiple-birth children (twins, triplets, etc.) have difficulties or delays in language which, 'indicates that the presence of two children of the same developmental age affects the quality of their experiences and communicative interactions' (Thorpe, 2006, p. 393). There may be many reasons for this, one of which Thorpe (ibid.) suggests could be that, 'the care demands are greater and reduce the time available for each individual child'. This research therefore suggests that we need to look to our settings and practice to ensure that vulnerable children have a greater opportunity for 1:1 and high quality interaction.

If we consider what Thorpe (2006) says about caring for children of the same developmental age having an impact, could this also be the rationale for considering the age demographics within our day nurseries, where the norm is to care for children of the same age in the same room? Should we not consider as I (Clare, 2012, p. 67) have advocated that

> by caring for children in a mixed age group, we are giving babies and young children the opportunity to experience their out-of-home care in a similar manner to the way they might be cared for at home along with their siblings, who will naturally be of different ages.

This concept was also advocated within the Millennium Cohort study report (Mathers et al., 2007), which suggests that when older children were present in a room, there was a better quality of interactions.

The toddler room is also where children and families come across the first stage of statutory assessment for education with the two year old progress check. As Communication and Language is one of the Prime Areas of Learning it is important that practitioners have a sound knowledge of where children's language should be; this, however, in keeping with the fact that children develop in different ways at different moments in time, should be assessment in its broadest terms.

Beyond the prime areas, it is for practitioners to decide what the written summary should include, reflecting the development level and needs of the individual child. The summary must highlight: areas in which a child is progressing well; areas in which some additional support might be needed; and focus particularly on any areas where there is a concern that a child may have a developmental delay. (DfE, 2014a, p. 13)

Jopling et al. (2013, p. 71) state that, 'children's facility for language at two years of age predicts their performance on entry to primary school' and it is with this in mind that we are now going to discuss typical language development for children between two and three years of age.

Typical development

One of the factors that has to be considered when looking at this age range is what is commonly called the 'terrible twos'; a stage which is universally recognised and one which causes issues not only for the toddler but any adult involved with them. We have all witnessed a scene, I am sure, where a frustrated (and often embarrassed) parent is trying to control a child who has thrown herself onto the floor and is screaming, when there is apparently no problem. Having recognised this, we then have to ask ourselves why these children are demonstrating this behaviour, and frustration is often the root cause. It is at this age that children are vocalising and there is nothing more frustrating than trying to make yourself understood when you think it is all so perfectly clear.

As discussed in Chapter 3, as children begin to vocalise their speech is not always clear. It is quite frequent for words to sound as if the toddler has a lisp as she says things like 'wabbit'. But this is a very exciting time when you consider that a typical two year old knows between 20 and 200 words and a typical three year old 1,000. This demonstrates how the language skills are rapidly developing in a child's third year; making it even more important that skilled practitioners' engagement with toddlers during this period of rapid growth and development is of the highest quality.

Along with this increase in vocabulary, children between two and three years of age are able to hold a real conversation where they apply the rules of grammar that they have listened to in the preceding two years. The sentences that they put together are simple two or three word sentences such as 'more bananas'.

As children's vocalising develops they are beginning to have a greater understanding of two-part commands, such as 'go to the shelf' and 'get a book'.

However, the use of longer requests from practitioners where children are asked to 'go to get your coat, put it on and then line up at the door' will result in children going to line up at the door, giving the impression that they are ignoring what they have been asked to do; whereas in fact the toddlers are just hearing the last part of the command.

There are times when the adults do not recognise the need to challenge children and move them on to the next level, as the following case study identifies.

Case study

Alfie is a child who first started at a day nursery because although his development was good, especially his spoken language, his mother felt that there was a need for him to socialise with other children away from her. He had begun to show distress if people or other children came to visit him in his home as it appeared that he resented anyone else sharing his mother with him.

When he first started at the nursery he was very withdrawn; he appeared to have adopted the role of observer before deciding to join in.

Alfie is very popular with the adults in the room; they appear to be fascinated by his language which is very good but they don't see the need to move this forward. They comment on his language but there is very little interaction of a high quality to extend him. The majority of Alfie's language and learning has come from home. This is evident in the way in which he approaches reading and the way in which he handles books. In many ways the practitioners failed Alfie as they did not help him to reach his potential. It was clear that he had a very good home learning environment but the practitioners did very little to move him on to the next level.

So what can the practitioner do to help these amazing skills and hopefully help children to overcome some of their frustrations? What can the practitioner do to challenge children's language development?

When looking at how adult involvement in activities can help and support toddlers' language and communication development it is important to link this to the EYFS *Outcomes* (DfE, 2013b). For this chapter we will be looking at the broad age bands 22–36 months (Table 4.1); I am also extending this focus to the Specific Area of Literacy to encompass reading and writing because, as we have seen, many children at this age have now become skilled in their communication skills and are beginning to show an awareness of print and communication across different media. Those statements which are in bold in Table 4.1 will be discussed in the Implications for Practice section which follows.

Table 4.1   Extracts from the EYFS *Outcomes* (DfE, 2013b) illustrating the discussions of the strands within the area of Communication and Language

	Listening and attention
22–36 months	**Listens with interest to the noises adults make when they read stories.**
	Recognises and responds to many familiar sounds (e.g. turning to a knock on the door, looking at or going to the door).
	Shows interest in play with sounds, songs and rhymes.
	Single-channelled attention. Can shift to a different task if attention fully obtained – using child's name helps focus.
	Understanding
22–36 months	**Identifies action words by pointing to the right picture (e.g. 'Who's jumping?').**
	Understands more complex sentences (e.g. 'Put your toys away and then we'll read a book').
	Understands 'who', 'what', 'where' in simple questions (e.g. Who's that? What's that? Where is?).
	Developing understanding of simple concepts (e.g. big/little).
	Speaking
22–36 months	Uses language as a powerful means of widening contacts, sharing feelings, experiences and thoughts.
	Holds a conversation, jumping from topic to topic.
	Learns new words very rapidly and is able to use them in communicating.
	Uses gestures, sometimes with limited talk, e.g. reaches towards toy, saying 'I have it'.
	Uses a variety of questions (e.g. 'What?', 'Where?', 'Who?').
	Uses simple sentences (e.g. 'Mummy gonna work').
	Beginning to use word endings (e.g. 'going', 'cats').
	Reading
22–36 months	**Has some favourite stories, rhymes, songs, poems or jingles.**
	Repeats words or phrases from familiar stories.
	Fills in the missing word or phrase in a known rhyme, story or game (e.g. 'Humpty Dumpty sat on a …').
	Writing
22–36 months	**Distinguishes between the different marks they make.**

Implications for practice

Questions and questioning

At this age children are beginning to ask simple questions as they explore and investigate their environments. To extend their questioning and thinking skills the practitioner needs to think carefully before inundating a child with questions that only require a Yes/No response. The following case study emphasises why this continuous questioning is not good practice.

Case study

As an Area SENCO (Special Educational Needs Consultant) I was asked by a playgroup to observe a child who they felt had some speech and language difficulties in that he was not beginning to put words together in simple sentences.

When I went into the room the boy in question was playing on his own in the 'small world' area; he was playing with the farm animals. I went into the area and sat down. He looked at me with what I can only say was an expression of annoyance as I think he felt I was coming to interrupt his play. I didn't say anything but he turned to me and then holding up the animals one at a time he said, 'cow', 'sheep', 'horse'. There was a look of disdain as he then returned to his play obviously thinking that he had given me what I had wanted! I turned to the adults and asked them whether anyone had ever engaged this boy in conversation or was it that they always asked him to name things? The failing here was that the adults were always bombarding children with questions – testing rather than supporting and extending.

Questions for reflection

Look at your own use of questioning within interactions by videoing yourself involved in either a child's play or in an adult-directed activity. View the video, reflecting on the following points:

- How many closed questions do you ask?
- How many open questions do you ask?
- How many turn taking opportunities are there?
- How many words are spoken by you?
- How many words are spoken by the child(ren)?

This exercise is useful because we are all unaware of how much in fact we dominate the talking space and how our use of questioning inhibits children from offering extended responses, demonstrating their use of vocabulary, grammar and thinking skills.

If we now return to the questioning that we do when we ask children to make a choice or decision, one of the things that we can do is to limit these options. Between the ages of two and three a child's often favoured word is *NO!* (This is not really that age-specific when we consider the petulant teenager!) In order to avoid a confrontation as a result of our questioning, if we restrict the offer then things become simpler.

Reflect on the following case study with this in mind.

Case study

Edward is two years old and he is attending a setting for the first time. He is overawed by the numbers of children and adults in the room and is feeling vulnerable, as his mother has left him for the first time since he has finished his gradual admission.

This vulnerable boy is then confronted by an environment which is similar to either a sweet or toy shop. The opportunities appear endless. His key adult approaches him and asks, 'What do you want to do?'. Should he go into the role play area and bake a cake for his mother? Should he go and build a wall like his father did at the weekend in the block play area? Should he go and curl up on a cushion in the book area to be on his own?

All these decisions to make in response to one simple question. What is he to do?

Reflect on this scene as a practitioner, putting yourself in the place of the child. If this was me I think I would freeze and stay silent. But consider the difference if the question had been, 'Do you want to climb a tree outside or bake a cake in the kitchen?'. This question makes the answer easier; all Edward has to say is 'Climb a tree'. The pressure has been taken off him and he can now begin to settle in under less traumatic conditions.

Extending and modelling

As stated at the beginning of this chapter, children of this age are beginning to utter two or three word sentences; we are now going to look at how as practitioners we can extend this skill. Before we move on we should reflect on those vulnerable children who are being targeted at the age of two through government funding. Murray et al. (2006, p. 234) highlight that children from low SES homes may experience more prohibitions and fewer affirmations. Prohibitions tend to be abrupt and contain very few models of an extended sentence structure. For example: *'Stop that!'*, *'No!'*, *'Get off!'*.

It is therefore incumbent on the practitioner to model good examples when interacting with toddlers. For example, if a child is playing with a 'baby' and says, 'Baby bed', the practitioner needs to respond positively at the same time as providing the child with of an example of how a sentence is framed: 'Yes let's put the baby to bed'.

As you can see, both the adult and the child are saying the same things but the adult version is giving the child a fuller picture of what is happening as well as offering the child a model for extending their sentence responses.

Narrating

Another useful tool in the practitioner's armoury is that of narrating. We have previously discussed (see Chapter 3) how sometimes toddlers need to be exposed to language models; narrating is another way of achieving this. When playing alongside a child we sometimes kill this play by trying to force ourselves in where we are not wanted. Instead, consider giving a narration of what you are doing. This could be, for example, explaining your actions as you roll out the dough and make a model or by telling a story as you play with the small world. This latter example often appeals to children, as you often see them telling similar stories when they are engaged with small world figures.

Narrating alongside a child to model an extended vocabulary and sentence structure is challenging children to move on to the next level or stage in their language development. This is reminiscent of Vygotsky's Zone of Proximal Development (ZPD) (1978), which he describes as the distance between the actual developmental level as determined by independent problem solving, and the level of potential development as determined through problem solving under adult guidance or in collaboration with more capable peers.

Rhyme and rhythm

A critical factor in developing and enhancing children's literacy development is through the use of rhyme and rhythm. This is supported by Kimura

(2006, p. 235) when she states, 'Music teaches toddlers that the world is a fun and exciting place to be as it strengthens their foundations of early literacy. Music enhances memory and develops important language skills'.

We have already seen how babies respond to the rhythmic sounds of 'motherese' as they tune into the mother's voice and sounds. This aware-ness of rhyme and rhythm needs to continue throughout infancy. Toddlers enjoy hearing and learning rhymes which lay the foundation for later phonic awareness. In order for children to segment the sounds of a word they first have to hear them. If as adults we play with words by making up alliterative or onomatopoeic sounds such as '*Splish, Splash, Splosh*', then toddlers will join in and begin to acquire this skill which is crucial for their later literacy development. 'Singing songs, playing with words or sounds, and reciting nursery rhymes all help children develop phonological sensi-tivity to the sounds of language, important skills that are related to later reading' (Notari-Syverson, 2006, p. 73).

On a personal note, when my grandson was born my daughter asked me what I wanted to be called and after long deliberation I decided on Grannie Annie; I was determined that I would give him an early start in hearing rhyme (this didn't quite work out as I'd carefully planned – see page 37)!

When talking about the use of rhymes, we mean that this is done by the adult in the room and not as a pre-recorded song – these do have their place, for example when used to support physical activity, but in general I personally believe that the disembodied voice loses personality and becomes less personal and individual for the child. Tape recordings lose the richness of a dialect; they almost appear to be perfect. The adult in the room, however, can adapt their pace, tone and actions to suit the children they are with.

Toddlers' reading and writing

When it comes to looking at reading and writing we are here thinking more about developing the skills that will ultimately enable children to perform these higher level functions. As we have already seen in this chapter the interaction and modelling by adults (parents and practitioners) is what gives toddlers the foundations for sentence structure, grammar and vocabulary. Research (Bradford and Wyse, 2013) tells us that engaging with writing and reading experiences early in life will help children to make connections in their learning and come to understand that print has a meaning.

As the home environment is where children get these first experiences it is important for parents to understand the importance of emergent writing, and that they are well informed about how to support and challenge their children.

So what do toddlers need to help them in their literacy journey and what can practitioners and parents do? One of the things that we know about young children is that they quickly begin to recognise the initial sound and letter of their own name; this is why many practitioners ask parents to help their child find their names as part of a self-registration system. This early recognition of letters can also be developed through the singing of the alphabet song. This type of activity recognises that alphabet knowledge is a predictor of later reading success Honig (2001).

Children also need to start associating the spoken language to the language of print and symbols. When looking at babies' development, children need to be read to on a regular basis so that they can begin to make links in their learning. The adult who shares a book with a toddler in a meaningful way gives them a growing love of books. The sharing of books should not be done in large groups as frequently seen in nurseries, but rather as an intimate process where there is quiet and time. The following points from Partridge (2004, p. 26) could be a useful checklist when looking at how books can and should be shared with children (this could also be worthwhile sharing with parents):

1. Establish a routine
2. Make reading an enjoyable experience
3. Read often
4. Reread favourite books
5. Bridge the language between the book and the child
6. Pay attention to the clues your child is giving you
7. Talk about the print
8. Read various types of books
9. Engage children in analytic talk
10. Encourage book-related play

Children of two years of age cannot sit for long periods, neither is it appropriate to read to large groups; if this is done in large groups then inevitably the adult will spend most of the time trying to maintain control. The use of small groups for activities is supported by the research of Elliott and Olliff (2008) when the size and length of circle time was adapted to no more than 10 minutes for two year olds with groups no larger than four to five children. Neither should books be shared as a 'fill-in' whilst the tables are set or children are taken to wash their hands. If we are to engage the young child in the pleasure of reading they need to be able to hear the story in its entirety. This way they will see that the story has a structure, as with all later writing and reading, of a beginning, a middle and an end.

The following two case studies of two boys between the ages of two and three demonstrate how reading and writing are inexorably linked. The two studies of Mark and Sam are taken from observations conducted over their second year, when Mark was in a day nursery and Sam was at home with his mother. Both of these boys had a love for books because books had been shared with them from birth. Mark was often seen as a 'naughty child' by the practitioners because they were unable to recognise his interests and thus challenge him.

Case study

Two years four months

- Mark appears distracted and heads to the mark making table. He twizzles the top of the pen, takes it off and then tries to put it on the end, he doesn't succeed but he is not bothered by this
- A girl joins him and says 'Here you are' as she gives him some paper. He makes some marks on the paper and then becomes fascinated again with the pen top as he tries to put it on and off
- He shows me a crayon, 'I've got a crayon'

Later in the observation ...

- Mark goes over to the books and begins to pull the books off the shelves looking for a particular book
- The adult gets it for him and he brings it to the table where I am sitting. It is a monster book. He has a pen and goes to write in it
- I give him a piece of paper and suggest that he writes on this instead
- He begins to draw, 'That's a monster'
- He looks at the pictures in the book, waves the paper back and forth and then says, 'That's Nicola' and he waves and smiles at the adult
- Mark makes marks on the paper for his monster, 'I've done that'. He is smiling as he looks around and stands next to me

(Continued)

(Continued)

Two years five months

- Mark begins to mark make on the paper. He is concentrating whilst he is doing this. He tells another boy that the 'Crayon's in there'
- Whilst mark making Mark makes circle movements and dots. He swaps the crayon from one hand to the other whilst he is making these marks. Mark selects another crayon and he whispers to himself as he does so. He takes his picture to the adult
- Mark then takes the crayons from one pot and then puts them back whilst looking at the other children having a story. He returns to putting the crayons into the pot
- He takes a picture to the adult to tell her that it is Ashley's
- He takes the picture to Ashley
- Mark puts the paper in the tray and carries some more away with him. He places the paper on a chair

Two years eight months

- Mark remembers that I have been there before and he asks me for a piece of paper from my pad and a friend gives him a crayon
- Mark babbles and chatters with his friend as he writes at the mark making table
- Mark makes a few marks on the paper. He holds the crayon in the appropriate way
- The adult says, 'Shall I draw with this one?'. Mark says 'No this one'
- The adult draws him a shape on a piece of paper but Mark is more interested in his own marks on the paper
- Mark turns to me and tells me that this is 'Ashley's shark'
- Ashley begins to colour in the shape that the adult has drawn for him but Mark is unconcerned by this and doesn't react
- Mark then turns his attention to his own paper
- Mark makes more marks on his piece of paper
- Mark tries to talk to the adult but she doesn't engage with him
- Mark tells her, 'I'm colouring in shark'

These observations of Mark show a boy who is interested in his own mark making. The adults don't seem to have recognised his interest in paper to use for mark making. I conducted these observations on a monthly basis, and Mark coming to ask me for paper was a common feature of my visits to the nursery.

Case study

The observations that I conducted on Sam began when he was seven days old and ceased when he was three. In Clare (2012) Sam's interest in books and associated activities are identified, as well as the influence and impact of having two older siblings to model higher levels of play and engagement.

[Rachel is Sam's mother and Megan his older sister.]

18 months

- Rachel asks Sam if he wants a pen like Megan. He takes one and he is given some paper. Rachel comments that he does enjoy this, but again it is prompted by seeing the others mark making. It is like modelling of early writing – it is always there if someone has got a pen – he just wouldn't look for one. It is generally prompted if the other two are doing something – like when they are painting or chalking
- Rachel tells me that Sam enjoys the chalk board and the white board – he likes being able to wipe it off and he will sit for minutes writing and then cleaning it off
- Sam's pencil hold is amazing – it is a proper pencil grip
- Rachel comments that his grip does change and that he has tended to hold it like that more recently. He is definitely right handed

19 months

Rachel comments that

> We have got a chalk board by the back door and that has been great as he will just go by that and write on it all the time. Because it is there and it is out – I counted the other day and he went to it about 15 times – as he goes past it he will pick up the chalk and use it.

Two years two months

- There is an obvious delight in reading the books and he interacts throughout, finishing the rhymes and pointing to pictures on the page. He chooses his own seating style and becomes absorbed in the books
- Some books he reads all the time

(Continued)

(Continued)

Two years four months

- Sam decides that he wants to go and choose a book; he goes next door to choose one. He brings in a book and says 'I going to read it' – it is a musical interactive book and he sits and reads with concentration. He sings along with the book – he isn't prompted to do this
- Rachel tells me that he likes singing when he chooses to. He will join in and sing along but he doesn't perform – he doesn't really join in at mother and toddlers but he will do it at home
- When he has finished with this book he goes off to get another book which he brings in for Rachel to read
- He has favourite books and favourite pages

Two years six months

- Rachel starts to read a book with him which has a definite rhyming pattern to it. Sam is enjoying the story and listens and responds to different parts of the story, finishing some of the rhymes. He asks to hear it again.

Two years nine months

On this occasion I go into the playgroup to observe Sam. He started to attend the group when he was two-and-a-half.

- When the book box comes out he goes to choose one – the older boy is there so Sam chooses a book for him. He eventually selects one for himself – *Spot the Dog*, lift and flap. He goes through the book to the end before getting up to ask to go to the toilet

Two years 10 months

- Another child asks what I am writing. Sam tells him that I am writing about him!!
- He then tells me that his t-shirt was wet and that this one has a frog on it:

  Can you write frog?

The following dialogue was interesting as it clearly demonstrates that Sam can see the link between the spoken and the written word

I got a bath upstairs. I eaten all of my cake. It is in my mouth. Yummy! I am having orange. Animals are coming out. Look there the animals. You write animals. Do you want orange. You write orange. You write cup. I just did a burp. A funny burp. You write animals [I show Sam that I have written animals] You write two animals. You write my tongue

Sam continues giving me things to write and I find it hard to keep up!

Another interesting feature of Sam's mark making, and indeed his adoption of the correct pencil grip at a very early age (18 months), is the tools that he had access to. As the younger sibling Sam is exposed to resources that wouldn't normally be accessible to such a young child, especially in a day care setting. He doesn't choose the chunky wax crayons, which are a feature of writing 'implements' for very young children in our settings; rather he selects the 'grown-up' pens and pencils.

Activity

Consider the 'literacy' resources that are offered to young children. Do we perhaps 'dumb' these down?

Tables for tracking children's involvement with books and their mark making activities

Tables 4.2 and 4.3 are ways in which it is suggested that practitioners could track children's involvement and development of their reading and mark making skills. These could be useful tools when writing up the two year old progress check and any other assessments.

Table 4.2   Record of children's involvement with books

Child's name	Context – Where?	Time – When?	Social – Who with?	Book read	Book chosen by?	Involvement

Table 4.3   Record of children's mark making activity

Child's name	Context – Where?	Time – When?	Tools chosen?	Child/adult initiated?	Involvement	Child's narration of what he has drawn

Questions for reflection

Using Tables 4.2 and 4.3 reflect on how you encourage toddlers to engage with books and how you respond to providing toddlers with a range of mark making activities to ensure that all children are involved.

Consider how you share information and guidance for parents to help them support and challenge their child's language development. For instance:

- Do you inform parents about the overuse of dummies?
- Do you give parents information about the nursery and action rhymes you use? (Remember that these may differ between cultures)
- Do you encourage parents to bring their child's favourite story into nursery?
- Do you give parents information about how to extend their children's language?
- Do you provide information about early mark making and its importance?

Further reading

- Rosenkoetter, S.E. and Knapp-Philo, J. (eds) *Learning to Read the World.* Washington DC: Zero to Three.

This book draws on research in the field of infant and toddler development as it relates to their language and literacy development. This is a large volume with chapters by different authors looking at the various aspects of language and literacy development in the first three years.

- Watch the videos by Colwyn Trevarthen on Language Development and Communication: www.educationscotland.gov.uk/learningandteaching/early learningandchildcare/prebirthtothree/nationalguidance/conversations/colwyntrevarthen.asp
- Partridge, H.A. (2004) 'Helping parents make the most of shared book reading', *Early Childhood Education Journal*, 32 (1): 25–30.

This short journal article describes a research study and some of the tools that were used in order to encourage and support parents when reading with their children. Some of the tools/activities used could prove useful for practitioners trying to get their parents involved with their child's literacy development.

- Watch the following video clip to see how important the early years are in relation to children's development: www.youtube.com/watch?v=M89VFIk4D-s

Of particular interest is the graph which shows the speed of development in the first two years.

5

Interaction and communication of children over three

This chapter will:

- Discuss children's development from three years until they start compulsory schooling
- Have a focus on the Specific Areas of learning of reading and writing
- Introduce a case study showing the progress of one boy's writing from three years' old
- Raise some challenging questions about the role of electronic devices

The children we are now going to look at are those in the three plus room, often referred to as the pre-school room. In the UK children can access maintained nursery school provision in the academic year in which they reach their fourth birthday and reception class when they are rising five. As a result of the structure of the UK's academic year some children will be starting nursery school when they are just three years old and reception when they are just four. This is in comparison with other systems (mainland Europe for instance) where children are not introduced to formal literacy learning systems until they are six or even seven years of age. This is highly relevant when one questions whether a child of three or four years of age is ready for this formal learning: physically, emotionally, cognitively and socially. For many it is too much, so it is incumbent on practitioners and other adults involved with children to ensure that they continue to build on the foundations that have been built, as discussed in the preceding chapters: storying, singing, listening, rhyming, sharing books.

It is also important when talking to parents about how they can support their children with their developing literacy skills that we encourage them not to become too formal too soon. We as practitioners will have had experience of parents, who though well intentioned, 'force' their children to engage with activities found in work books that are inappropriate. As Leach (2011, p. 26) points out, 'Babies and toddlers don't need adults to *teach* them, but they do need to help them learn'.

Practitioners in the pre-school and following nursery and reception years are under pressure from the government: 11 out of the 17 Early Learning Goals (ELGs) in 2014 involve literacy. This is in addition to pressure from parents who, because they are aware of the importance of reading and writing, push for their child's early acquisition of these skills.

What practitioners need is knowledge and understanding of the complexities of literacy acquisition and how to make it relevant and fun (Brock and Rankin, 2008).

As discussed throughout this book, the first thing that practitioners and parents need to be are good role models. If children do not see adults browsing a range of different reading materials (books, letters, newspapers, information leaflets, etc.) and writing for a variety of purposes, they quite understandably don't see the relevance of acquiring these skills. In this digital age this is more important than ever before. How many of us communicate through texting and social media on our phones? How many of us use a range of devices to write, whereas in the past we used pens and paper for most of our written communication?

So how can we 'grab' the young child's openness and show them that reading is fun. First is to have relevance. All children are different. Out of my three children the two girls loved a fictional bed-time story but these did not appeal to my plane-crazy son; they had no relevance for him. They just did not 'speak to him'. This is how for the bed-time story I found myself reading the workings of the jet propelled engine, not really understanding what I was reading but noticing his sheer pleasure in the words.

So how do we know when a child is ready for reading or for starting to make sense of the written word? A child's initial foray into this area is when they become interested in their own names, showing excitement when they spot the initial letter of their name in other words. As adults have shared books with them since birth they have acquired the knowledge that the funny squiggles on a page represent the words being spoken. They might start looking for their initial, or they might start to ask what the sign in the shop means. These are signals that a child might be ready to begin to break down the phonic sounds within a word.

Children, who have been read to regularly, with stories repeated many times, will astound parents and practitioners as they begin to tell a much-loved story word for word, as demonstrated in the following case study.

Case study

The Bad Tempered Ladybird (Carle, 2010) has been read to Lucy many times and it has become a much-loved book. One night as her mother settles her down for her usual bed-time story, Lucy asks if she can be the mummy tonight. She instructs her mother to lie in the bed as she takes on the adult role and position. She holds the book imitating her mother's practice. She then proceeds to tell the story.

This rendition is nearly word perfect and in synchrony with the pages. She turns the pages over keeping them in pace with her story telling.

Lucy's mother is amazed; previously Lucy had just echoed some of the line endings. When the story is finished Lucy is smiling, very proud of herself. Good self-esteem. As for her mother, well she is so proud of her literate daughter.

This scene will be very familiar to parents and practitioners as would the times when the parent or practitioner is tired and tries to skip a few pages in a familiar story. As Crystal (2011, p. 46) reminds us when he states, 'I thought it wouldn't be noticed if I made it "The Two Little Pigs." Not a chance. I got a severe telling off, and had to start the story all over again, paying special attention to the house of twigs'.

Questions for reflection

This scenario can only happen if the atmosphere is right and the foundations have been laid. Consider whether in your setting a situation like this could occur.

(Continued)

(Continued)

Ask yourself the following questions:

- Do we create the right atmosphere?
- Do we repeat stories enough?
- Are the books we are sharing with children of a high enough quality?
- Do our books have good rhyme and pattern?
- Is the environment a listening one?
- Can we create situations for individual children to express their reading abilities?

The following case study is of an observation I made in a private day nursery and is an example of a practitioner who has got it right.

Case study

The small group of children have come in from outside and they ask the adult if they can have a story. The adult settles the children in the small cosy book area and then turns the main light off. She draws the canopy closed around the children and then switches on the fairy lights which are scattered over the top. This creates a magical moment and the children all fall quiet as they settle down to listen. The children stay engaged with the story until the end.

When it is over they go into the rest of the room except for one girl who asks the adult if they can read a bed-time story. Making some minor adjustments to the furniture and getting a blanket, the adult and the child snuggle in for a very special story.

This case study demonstrates how the practitioner can engage children in reading; this also shows how story telling does not always have to be in formal groups, where children are once again bombarded with questions about the book – questions which are unimaginative and which tend to get monosyllabic responses from the children. In the training programme *Communication Matters* (DfES, 2005) there is a video clip of a teacher sitting with a small group of children to talk about 'Goldilocks and the

Three Bears'. Her voice dominates the talking space and the children are not engaged; when the practitioner reflected on this session by watching the video she was astounded and sought to rectify what she saw as her mistakes. In the next clip she can be seen to let the children take the lead in the discussion – relating to their own experiences. On this occasion it was the children who dominated the talking space; the adult was merely a facilitator and observer.

The *Communication Matters* training pack identified 10 key questions for practitioners to use to reflect on how their own language and behaviour can have an impact on the development of children's communication and language. Practitioners need to reflect on their practice by taking these questions and thinking about how often they:

1. Listen to children before they talk to them?
2. Allow children time to start up the conversation?
3. Find themselves regularly interrupting children?
4. Talk with a child rather than at them?
5. Leap in to correct children's errors or ask children to repeat themselves?
6. Ask too many questions of children, particularly those to which the answers are already known?
7. Model and expand children's language, building on what they have to say?
8. Feel uncomfortable about silences?
9. Show real interest in what children have to say?
10. Show the same respect for conversations with children as for those with adults?

(www.literacytrust.org.uk/talk_to_your_baby/news/1612_mind_your_language)

Vocabulary

As children experience the world and what is in it, so their vocabulary develops and increases. Through the books that they have shared and read they come across words which help them to communicate with a range of audiences. I often find that practitioners are in danger of 'talking down' to children, always giving them simplified versions of words when in fact if children hear a range of vocabulary they are able to extend their vocal communication. The following case study is an example of how children's language and vocabulary can be developed and thus enhanced through having first-hand experiences.

Beach case study

(With thanks to Ruth Holland, MA)

The following case study was part of some action research conducted in one Local Authority in 2007. The main purpose of the research was to establish whether first-hand experiences such as visiting a beach could contribute significantly to improving young children's language development.

The rationale behind the project was that in 2007 more than 57.3% of children scored six or more for Communication, Language and Literacy Development (CLLD) and Personal, Social and Emotional development (PSED) in their Foundation Stage Profile (FSP) assessments. The gap between these children and those whose scores were in the lowest 20% had not improved. There was a need, therefore, to employ strategies that would serve to narrow this gap in achievement.

So what happened ...?

- The pupils in the reception classes of the primary school with the lowest CLLD Foundation Stage Profile score within the Local Authority in 2007 were identified as the target group of children to work with. A parallel class in a neighbouring school with a similar intake of children were also selected as a control group.
- In order to ascertain whether the action taken had any impact on the children's vocabulary, both groups of children were given an informal vocabulary test (The Renfrew Action Picture Test, Catherine Renfrew, 2010) devised to fit the proposed trip. A balance of nouns, verbs and adjectives was used as well as some high frequency words and some low frequency words
- The control group of children were to be given experiences within their school related to a beach experience. The teacher did an excellent job of recreating this experience by converting the concrete playground into a beach, covering the entire space with sand and giving children tools so they could experience it as they would as if they were on a beach. The children were told to come dressed for a beach experience; on one day they were visited by an ice cream van where they could go and get their ices. Inside the classroom the teacher had recreated beach scenes with the 'small world' and offered hands-on tactile experiences with natural materials and supporting resources such as books.

- The research group were taken with their parents to a beach on a coach; there they went paddling in the sea, flew home-made kites on the sandbanks and went up a lighthouse. For most of these children this was their first experience of a beach; this was also true for some of the parents accompanying their children.

Figures 5.1 and 5.2 demonstrate the difference in scores on assessment in relation to children's vocabulary. The results show improved use of language in both cohorts with a greater increase for the research group.

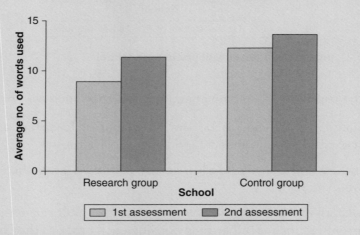

Figure 5.1   Increase in vocabulary in each school

- The total vocabulary scores improved for the research group and increased from 178 to 247. This represented an average increase from 8.9 to 12.35.
- The total vocabulary scores improved for the control group from 206 to 246. This represented an average increase from 11.44 to 13.67.
- The average age equivalency improved for research group from four years 11 months to five years 11 months.
- The average age equivalency improved for the control group from five years three months to six years.

(Continued)

(Continued)

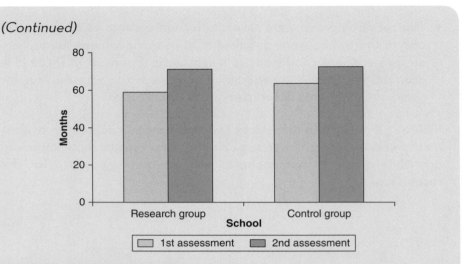

Figure 5.2   Increase in age equivalency in each school

After the trip there was some anecdotal evidence such as:

I noticed, 'lighthouse', to be the word that children appeared most excited about. (Speech and Language Therapist)

I paddled and put my hand in sea and found a crab shell and seaweed. (Child)

When talking about their favourite bit the children all gave different responses rather than copying each other as they often do. (Class Teacher)

This project demonstrates how giving children first-hand experiences can have an impact on their vocabulary.

Questions for reflection

- Consider ways in which you could improve children's vocabulary by offering them first-hand experiences.
- If first-hand experiences are not possible due to a number of factors including opportunity and economics, consider how, just as the teacher did in the control group, you can make the experiences exciting and meaningful for children.

- The parents in this piece of action research accompanied their children so that they could share in the experience. What would you consider to be the benefits to children's language development of parents sharing in such experiences?
- Look at your use of vocabulary; do you think that you challenge children by offering them models of 'sophisticated' language?

Writing

One thing we have to remember when talking about children learning to read and write in English is the complexity of our language. The English alphabet has 26 letters but there are over 40 sounds when spoken. This then gets even more complicated when children encounter those squiggles on the page – writing or print. Here they are introduced to upper and lower case, in print to the vast range of fonts available and finally to the vagaries of handwriting.

The child learning to read has to overcome all of these obstacles in order to be termed literate. But here we come across the increasing dependency on electronic devices for writing. Part of being considered literate is the ability to communicate in an agreed format that is understandable by all. We have to spell; in a book this is done for us and to a certain degree computer systems will correct inaccuracies, but they won't find them all. With the increasing use of text talk, children, and increasingly adults, use text spelling, which for someone of my age is hard to decipher unless I spell it out in my head. I was recently shocked by a text message from my youngest daughter (a doctor) when she asked if she had left her 'ballballs' (baubles) at her sister's house! At least this was phonetically correct! Digital literacy is a subject we will return to at the end of this chapter.

The following case study was something that emerged from a conversation with a colleague who had a four year old son.

Case study

We were discussing early writing in relation to some training we were doing together when she commented that Fin, her son, didn't appear to see the purpose of writing; we examined this and came up with three questions. Was it because he was:

(Continued)

(Continued)

1. A boy?
2. Not interested in print in general?
3. Not given role models for writing?

We concluded that the second question did not apply in this case as Fin was an avid 'reader' of books and stories, mainly due to his mother's passion for the written word. As a consequence his spoken language and vocabulary were excellent. The answer to the first question was more difficult to answer. Historically, research has told us that in the area of literacy, as measured by the Early Years Foundation Stage Profile (EYFSP), at the end of the reception year girls outperform boys especially when looking at the outcomes for writing: 'a larger proportion of girls at this stage of education are able to write for a variety of purposes, use phonics knowledge to write simple regular words and make phonetically plausible attempts at more complex words' (Bourke and Adams, 2011, p. 250). This could be for a range of reasons, from boys having looser upper body muscle tone which needs to be developed before they can engage in the fine motor skill of writing, to the high targets which are expected from children at the age of five.

The last question, however, was the one that provoked the deepest discussion. Do we, as adults in this age of technology, model writing to our youngest children? Having worked as a local authority consultant for over 14 years and having visited numerous settings I would say that I have seen very little modelling of writing in settings, except when adults are writing observations. But this too is changing as many settings are turning to iPads and electronic systems to record these observations.

In our discussion we then turned to the home. A question we need to ask ourselves is how often do we write in the traditional way at home? I asked my daughter this question and she replied that as a minimum she does write a shopping list; this in fact is true but as I witnessed later in the week this list was 'written' on her phone! Again we need to ask the question, how often do we write and receive letters?

I recently went to a dear friend's mother's funeral and one of the key parts of the eulogy and subsequent reminiscences of her life was that she wrote people beautiful letters and they remembered them. I certainly remember the one she wrote to my youngest daughter following a serious bicycle accident.

So where did this lead us in our discussion of Fin's writing? Well I started to write letters to him and I posted them. What follows are Fin's letters to me over the years in chronological order.

Figure 5.3(a) **May 2012**

Figure 5.3(b) **June 2012**

(Continued)

(Continued)

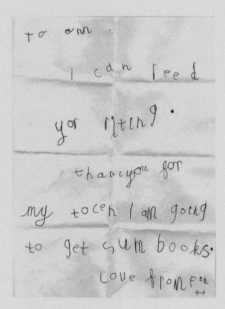

Figure 5.3(c)   October 2012

Figure 5.3(d)   January 2013

Figure 5.3(e)   April 2013

Figure 5.3(f)   May 2013

(Continued)

(Continued)

Der ann
where have you
been ann?. Is the Zoo
or the animal
parck? Sam and Erin
and Jess and Jonah
I Went to & sale.
Lo J Zure Centert
I played games.
I liked the Punching
bags & bea cos I lwk
to Punch. Love From Fin

Figure 5.3(g)   June 2013

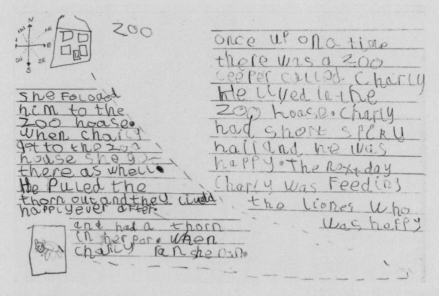

Figure 5.3(h)   June 2013

You will notice that as time went by Fin's writing development is quite clear. This development has turned Fin into a writer who sees a purpose to learning this skill. To this day we still exchange letters and postcards and I have begun the process with my grandson, Oscar, in the hope that this will engage him with writing.

The modelling of writing for a purpose is something which needs to be practised within settings.

Questions for reflection

Consider how and when you model writing for children. Do you demonstrate the importance of writing in your life to the children in your care? Could you perhaps develop a similar long term project, such as writing and receiving letters, with the children?

Digital literacy

I would now like to return to something that was mentioned in the introduction to the previous case study: digital literacy. This could be defined as the knowledge, skills and behaviours used in a broad range of digital devices such as smartphones, tablets, laptops and desktop PCs, all of which are seen as network rather than computing devices; but for our purposes I feel that we need to look at how perhaps having these digital skills can and possibly is having an impact on the more traditional forms of literacy, such as reading and writing.

I am not a Luddite as I embrace all forms of digital communication – from Facebook to emails to a Kindle. To a certain extent this embracing of digital media is easier for me as I have had a lifetime cementing my literacy skills in the traditional manner. For young children today, however, this is more complex, as although they see the adults in their lives using these tools they are constantly being told that it is bad for them to use them as they are too young.

Digital tools are now very much part of our everyday lives and so it is not amazing that children are exposed to them from a very early age. We can often see this acquired knowledge when we see babies imitating their parents by scrolling screens; in fact I have also seen older people trying to scroll pages of magazines! And so these tools have become assimilated into our everyday lives; we use them to gather information and to communicate – ways of interacting that traditionally have been done through the spoken voice or by the written word. So what does this mean for the literacy development of our very youngest children? I personally feel that these tools should be used alongside the traditional modes of communication, thus embracing all technologies to help us communicate. I read books using a tablet, therefore should digital books be included in children's libraries? Many people would find this concept abhorrent, and yet didn't we in the early years embrace the use of voice-recorded audio-books because we felt that this could be a way of engaging with those children who were reluctant readers.

The issue facing schools and early years educators is a step change in the way in which they regard the skill of reading. In modern-day culture it is apparent schools and indeed early years settings have to alter their perception that printed text is the primary means of communication (Marsh cited in Hall, 2003).

Rachel Levy (2009) in her small scale study involving 12 children aged from three to six looked at the ways in which they were engaging with screen text and how they used a variety of strategies to make sense of the range of symbols, including print. Levy found that although the children could not necessarily interpret the print they knew what the symbols represented and could act accordingly.

If we take this as a starting premise, where should practitioners take the use of digital communication into their practice? As previously stated, children are already familiar with this form of communication from their experiences at home and in the wider community; they see how tablets and phones are used by their parents and increasingly they are exposed to symbols instead of print within the wider community. The work of Yamada-Rice (2010) clearly demonstrates the impact that the visual mode has on the lives of young children. Even though it is recognised that children are exposed to digital media within their homes, parents are, as yet, still concerned about the amount of time that young children have access to them, especially when they are met with headlines telling them of the dangers of children having too much 'on-screen' time: '*Are iPads and tablets bad for young children?*' (Cocozza, 2014). This dilemma means that parents are caught in the crossfire between empowering their children's technological learning or causing them danger from an unknown harm.

This concern about the overuse of digital experiences is also felt within the practice of many early years practitioners. But is this the only concern? I feel that many of the restrictions on the use of digital tools to enhance literacy are barriers of finance and self-confidence. The economics factor is a very clear one; as technology evolves at a rapid pace it is very difficult for settings and schools to keep up with the pace of change with their limited budgets. When I visit settings today I am amazed at the many desktop computers that I see on offer to the children – an offer which many children now reject as they are no longer familiar with the mouse and the key board. What children need and have experience of is the touch screen which gives them an immediate response. I don't necessarily agree with the instant gratification that today's young children are experiencing but I do agree that the technology that we offer them in settings has to be the most up to date – a difficult thing to achieve with ever-diminishing budgets.

My next challenge is to practitioners themselves. How many of us reject the use of these tools because we ourselves are not comfortable or confident in their use? How many of us see the relevance of young children engaging with these resources? And yet, I have seen practice where confident practitioners have used tablets to great effect – where they are used in small groups so as to enhance children's social skills as well as their Information and Communications Technology (ICT) and literacy skills.

What practitioners need to know about is the research (Neumann, 2014, p. 119) that tells us that there is a 'positive association detected between children's access to tablets, name writing and letter sound knowledge … [indicating] that the tactile nature of tablets may play a role in the acquisition of these skills'. The tactile nature of the touch screen links in with everything we know about how children learn and develop through experiences, especially those of a tactile nature.

What I think of as more of a challenge is the way in which children's literacy skills will change and evolve as tablets, iPads, etc., become more commonly used within the education system. There are already schools which are 'paper free', where children are using digital technology to record all of their work and where sometimes (mainly in secondary education) children are being 'taught' in a lecture-style fashion through these media. There are some questions that I would like to raise in relation to this (and as a challenge for future research):

1. Does this evolution of the digital age mean that our children will no longer need to learn to write?
2. Does the way in which children interact with the touch screen through symbols mean that there will not be such a demand for 'reading' in the traditional manner?
3. Is this the way in which our communication and language will evolve, just as it has since Chaucer's writing of *The Canterbury Tales* where he wrote:

Whan that aprill with his shoures soote
The droghte of march hath perced to the roote,
And bathed every veyne in swich licour
Of which vertu engendred is the flour;

Which is translated into modern English as:

When the sweet showers of April have pierced
The drought of March, and pierced it to the root,
And every vein is bathed in that moisture
Whose quickening force will engender the flower

(Chaucer, Geoffrey and Coghill, 2003, p. 3)

Questions for reflection

Whilst reflecting on the evolution of language as discussed earlier, consider how the language you use has changed and what impact this may have on the way in which you communicate both verbally and in writing with the children that you work with.

- Can you see a time when children will not need to write? What can you do to ensure that young children are still motivated to write?
- How can you embrace traditional and digital forms of communication so that they complement each other?
- Consider how you use digital technology in your practice to support children's emergent literacy through symbols, stories and mark making.
- What barriers exist within your setting to the development of the use of digital technology? Consider how these could be overcome.

Before concluding this chapter I would like to include a section on alternative communication, which is a case study prompted by an observation on a train journey.

Case study

A child of about three or four years of age got on the train with her mother; she was chatting away and appeared to be excited to be going on a journey. They sat on either side of one of the tables and began to look out of the window. I did not want to stare so I was looking straight ahead but out of the corner of my eye I saw that the child was making a lot of movement with her arms and that she frequently turned to look at her mother, telling her about the things that she was seeing out of the window and pointing them out – nothing out of the ordinary, except that it struck me as odd that the mother was not responding verbally to the little girl. Curiosity got the better of me and I turned to have a look; what I saw both surprised and delighted me.

The reason that the little girl was using a lot of hand and arm movements as well as turning to face her mother was that she was signing to her. This accounted for the lack of a verbal response from the mother, who was obviously deaf and communicated with her daughter through sign language.

What I loved about this scene was the girl's movements; her hands appeared to be very expressive and there was a graceful fluidity about the way in which she held a conversation with her mother. If I was to look at this child's emotional well-being I would say that she was scoring highly; her whole body appeared at ease and there was a joy in her facial as well as her hand expression. What was also very important was the eye contact; this not only meant that the two could communicate but it was also affirmation to the little girl that what she had to say was important and that the mother was interested and wanted to be part of the excitement.

Further reading

- Brock, A. and Rankin, C. (2008) *Communication, Language and Literacy from Birth to Five*. London: Sage Publications.

This book gives an overview of children's communication, language and literacy. Relevant to this section is Chapter 7, which focuses on emerging literacy and how it can be promoted through activities and experiences.

- Neumann, M. (2014) 'An examination of touch screen tablets and emergent literacy in Australian pre-school children', *Australian Journal of Education*, 58 (2): 109–122, doi: 10.1177/0004944114523368.

This interesting research, based in Australia, looks closely at the views of parents on their young children's use of tablets as well as looking at the relationships between their use and emergent literacy skills.

• Crystal, D. (2011) *A Little Book of Language*. New Haven and London: Yale University Press.

Crystal is an expert linguist and this book gives on insight into the story of language. Crystal writes in an enlightening manner, making the subject informative as well as entertaining and relevant.

6

Bilingualism in the early years

This chapter will:

- Consider the impact that acquiring a second language has on a child's acquisition of his first language
- Discuss the analysis and findings from a small scale research study

So far we have been looking at the way in which normally developing children acquire language, their native language. But in our multi-ethnic society many children are exposed to two languages from birth or from when they begin to access a day care setting.

Background

Having been a local authority early years consultant for many years I have worked in both the maintained and non-maintained sectors and I have encountered children with English as an Additional Language (EAL). As a moderator of the Early Years Foundation Stage Profile (EYFSP) I was accustomed to analysing data to look for patterns taking into account such factors as the number of children on free schools meals (FSM), the number of children with special educational needs (SEN), the number of summer born children, the number of boys in relation to girls and the number of children with EAL. When analysing data (and when talking to heads, teachers and practitioners in the UK) there are some concerns that in the UK we view children who are acquiring a second language in a negative way, and perhaps a deficit model is being worked in and experienced. Why should this be? In reporting one study, Michael-Luna (2013, p. 447) states, 'The disproportionate number of referrals of English learners for Special Education service … suggests that teachers may not be distinguishing language development from cognitive development'.

Another factor within this is that children who have EAL must be assessed for the EYFSP as follows:

> Within the EYFS Profile, the ELGs for communication and language and for literacy must be assessed in relation to the child's competency in English. The remaining ELGs may be assessed in the context of any language – including the child's home language and English. (DfE, 2014b)

This obviously puts some children at a very early disadvantage, as although they may be competent and confident in their first language they are being assessed on their development in their second language.

Are teachers also influenced by the fact that 11 out of the 17 Early Learning Goals (ELGs) involve spoken language? Does this not tend to ensure that these children are seen as not achieving despite the government's standpoint that 'learning English as an additional language is not a special educational need' (ibid., p. 15).

Our own personal experiences will play a huge part here. And so before we begin to look at the complexities of acquiring two languages I want to state my positionality here. One of the reasons for wanting to write this book was my desire to know more about bilingual speakers in the early years. I have a grandson, Oscar (who you will have met through various case studies), who went to live in Munich, Germany, when he was nine months old and who began to attend a German Krippe (similar to an English pre-school) when aged 18 months for four mornings a week and who is now, at the age of three, considered to be bilingual.

I begin by first questioning my views in relation to my grandson: do I consider this second language acquisition a good thing because I am so-called 'middle class' and think that any 'extra' learning is a bonus, but then why don't teachers in the UK consider it a bonus in their schools? Is it because my grandson's first language is English, the language that pre-dominates across the world? Is it because Oscar's second language is a first world European language? Is it that in his Krippe some of the teachers are fluent English speakers whereas in this country there are limited numbers who speak the diverse range of languages that may appear in our schools (Gujarati, Punjabi, Polish, Romanian, Zulu, Russian, French and Swedish, to name just a few that I have come across).

Activity

Reflect on your own professional thoughts about children who speak different languages in your setting and the implications for practitioners, families and most importantly for children.

Babies' ability to acquire a second language

By understanding the development implications for bilingual babies and children we can begin to further understand why negative assumptions about learners with EAL are made.

As babies develop there appears to be a critical or sensitive period when it is easier to acquire a second language. This is a time when the sounds that have not been heard will be pruned. Pruning refers to the way in which the brain develops. As babies and young children experience things in their world, connections are formed and with repeated use these connections become stronger; those connections which are not used repeatedly will become weaker and fade away making the brain circuits more efficient. (Useful videos on brain development can be found at: http://developingchild.harvard.edu/index.php/resources/multimedia/videos/three_core_concepts/.) This process is called pruning. We all know the stereotypical jokes about how the Japanese have difficulty saying 'fried rice' as they tend to say 'flied lice'; this is because the 'r' sound does not exist in the Japanese language and so is pruned. Why would they need to retain this sound when within their culture this sound is redundant? What is interesting to consider is exactly when does a Japanese baby learn that in her language it doesn't matter whether she produces 'r' or 'l' because the adults in her culture can't hear the difference anyway and it won't change the meaning of the word in Japanese? (Gopnik et al., 2001, p. 106).

Young children who are exposed to more than one language have to contend with learning not only the words/labels for each language but they also need to begin to understand how the grammar of each language works. As we know, children begin to understand the mechanics of a language by listening to sentence structures and apply the heard rules within their speech. So for instance we often hear young children in their early speech making what we consider to be mistakes when they say such things as 'I have got two foots' or 'I felled over'. Whilst this isn't correct, if you stop and consider the complexities of the English language you will see that theoretically the child has applied grammatical rules to construct these phrases. They have listened and they have 'absorbed' the fact that in English plurals end with an 's' and past tenses in 'ed'. What they haven't learnt yet is that in English there are exceptions to every rule! So how much harder is this for the children who are not only acquiring the words to talk but also the grammatical structure of two languages (Fennell et al., 2007)? As Conteh (2012, p. 27) explains, children need to know about grammar; but the grammar will only make sense to them when they can relate it to real texts.

Because very young children learn their vocabulary and grammar through conversation in their native language, the skills required to do this in two languages give them advantages over their monolingual peers. As Siegal et al. (2010) explain, 'Bilingualism has been found to have a positive effect on children's ability to judge grammar and to substitute symbols. In this sense, exposure to more than one language appears to facilitate children's metalinguistic awareness'.

It has been well established that by the age of nine months, infants can learn from exposure to a foreign language in natural infant-directed conversations (Kuhl, 2004). The important point here is the use of the word *conversations* which implies a personal interaction – something which occurs face to face. This demonstrates the vital role that practitioners play in developing the vocabularies of children acquiring a second language, and is also an important reminder that this acquisition will not occur if things are presented through the mediums of television and audiotapes (Kuhl, 2004).

Studies have shown that compared with monolingual children, bilingual children pass their development milestones at similar ages. Is this because they are open and receptive, that they have this strong urge to communicate or that their brains are particularly 'plastic' enough to take on this complexity?

In an interesting study Byers-Heinlein et al. (2010) concluded that the same processes that support language acquisition in a child's native language, such as listening, are also used to support the acquisition of a second language. This study stressed the importance of rhythm as one of these processes, and one which may have an impact on the way in which children go on to acquire a second language. In other words, for the young bilingual speaker we need to ensure that they are having the same experiences as their monolingual equivalent.

What is also of interest is that Byers-Heinlein et al. argue that babies who are exposed to 'two languages throughout gestation have already begun the process of bilingual acquisition at birth' (2010, p. 347). As can be seen in our earlier discussions babies are already listening to voices and language in the womb, therefore we have to assume that in a multi-lingual environment the baby has already been exposed to the sounds of the different languages. This poses a challenging thought when we later look at the acquisition of a second language by young children who have moved to a non-native language speaking environment, such as my grandson and the other children who we shall meet later in this chapter. Are children who move to a different language environment already equipped to take on a second language because they have previously been exposed to quality language experiences, or are they at a disadvantage because they have not heard the different languages spoken whilst in the womb?

Small scale research study – practitioners' perspectives

When I conducted my small scale research study I was interested in getting the views of both parents and practitioners about how the acquisition of a second language in the early years affects their practice and their relationships, as well as what impact this acquisition has on the child.

In the questionnaires and in the interviews that I conducted with the practitioners there were some commonalities in the responses. In line with the research already discussed they felt that immersing children in the second language was most effective with very young children and its effectiveness decreased with older children. Some of the practitioners referred to the subject of total immersion in a language within a setting whilst maintaining their native language within the home. One practitioner working in a German setting stated:

> some children have absolutely no problems at all with the language and I think some children are linguistically competent, they are very empathic with the way they learn things, they have no problems, they can deal with the immersion system and dealing with the language being German and somehow they'll pick it up.

This empathetic acceptance of being immersed in a second language by practitioners working outside of the UK, appears to be different from the opinion of another practitioner working in Europe, who gives a picture of children attending her setting as being isolated, 'he was playing in the playground and babbling away to the children but no one was really responsive back, and you can tell he's desperate for that, and he's trying his hardest'.

This practitioner also confirmed my own concerns about UK settings with regard to their acknowledgement, or as in this instance, lack of acknowledgement, that second language acquisition is an asset and not a special need. A common reaction to bilingualism in the UK is, as one practitioner described it to me:

> Hand on heart, dead honest … when we actually looked at how many different languages there are on site our initial response was, gosh! Not look at all this enriched culture, look at all this that we could be learning from each other, it was gosh, how are we going to cope?

It has to be borne in mind that this is the opinion of one practitioner but this comment came about as part of a frank and open discussion where she also stated that she felt that they had this reaction because of the way in which they are judged and monitored by regulatory bodies; they have to show progression and some of these children might only be in the setting for six months for 10 hours a week, before they attend mainstream nursery school, which is a very short period of time. This view about the assessment and regulatory bodies is echoed by Michael-Luna (2013) when he describes the difficulties teachers face because of the policy drive for assessment within the early years.

Total immersion was also commented on by a Danish practitioner who discussed her setting's policy on total immersion as an enforceable one, 'Our school has adopted a "Speak English at School" policy with signs posted around to remind kids to speak English and an award given at assembly time to the classroom found speaking the most English'. She goes on to comment that from her personal perspective, and that of some of the parents, that this is promoting a negative atmosphere within the school. I think this is a challenging thought, especially after hearing the positive comments from those practitioners who work in total immersion settings. Is this about creating a balance? If so does that make it even more confusing for those children who are experiencing difficulties in acquiring the two languages side by side? Is it this acquisition that is the key? This enforceable 'banning' of the native language is reminiscent of the 'Welsh Not' policy of a native language as a disorder, as described by Aldridge and Waddon (1995, p. 205):

> bilingualism was often considered a disorder that could be corrected by pushing all traces of the invading language out of the inflicted child.

This remedy was imposed despite the fact that the unwanted language was often the language of the child's home, heritage and tradition. An invidious example of this was the 'Welsh Not'. This was a piece of wood on a cord worn around the neck by schoolchildren in Wales in the Victorian era if they were caught speaking Welsh at school. The bearer of the Not was subjected to degrees of punishment based on how long it had been worn before being passed on to the next 'offending' child.

As already stated, the general consensus of opinion from the small scale study was that the introduction to or immersion in a second language is better the younger the child. Two practitioners sum this up succinctly when they state:

> I have found that if children start when they have already turned two and they have never encountered English before, then I think it is a bit weird for them to be exposed to a new language.

And:

> If they come in at two-and-a-half it can be more difficult because a lot of children are then competent in their language skills.

Other practitioners talked about younger children picking up the second language faster, being more flexible, accepting things naturally, being less anxious about making mistakes, having brains which are still developing and making connections and because, 'their means of communication is not solely verbal'.

This latter statement is for me quite thought provoking, especially when you consider that children have been exposed to language since conception and have already begun to formulate language in their native tongue; it is the sounds of this language which have begun to make those vital connections in the brain. In the UK the political drive (Field, 2010; Allen, 2011) to prevent children having a poor start in their learning means the government is funding places for disadvantaged two year olds. Perhaps there should be some political thought given to making access to provision for children without English to attend as early as possible, probably from about 18 months. This would surely mean that we could prevent the acquisition of a second language being viewed within a deficit model as the children move through the educational phases. This is not to say that I think all children should start in a total immersion system as early as possible, but I do think it is worth considering making this available for the growing numbers of children with EAL accessing the English education system.

My main concern with an early start for all children is the impact that this could potentially have on their emotional well-being. Having said this, from the comments of practitioners, the earlier children are exposed to the second language the less of an impact on their emotional well-being:

> I think being immersed into a foreign language environment always has an impact on the emotional well-being of a child. However, the impact of this is far greater on an older child than a younger one who is still learning language and is much more open to new experiences and less inhibited.

There was a consensus among the small group involved in the research project that by exposing children to the second language as early as possible there was a positive impact on those children's emotional well-being. Practitioners talked about children who were exposed to a second language later as being isolated, in their own bubble, frustrated, alienated, all words which when we apply them to children are very worrying. This is why the relationship between the setting and parents is of vital importance.

The role of parents

Research (Sylva et al., 2003) has shown that the influence of parents on the child's learning and development is vital, and nowhere of greater importance than in language development through everyday interaction and communication with their child. If the parents' role is considered crucial, then the relationships that they establish with their child's key person and other adults is essential so that they can continue with this support. This becomes more difficult when the setting and the parents do not have a common language. Practitioners recognise this difficulty when they state such things as: 'One of our major things to work on is bringing people in, and we can't get them in because there is such a language barrier' and 'relationships between parents and practitioners are so important, especially during the settling in phase, and I think language and communication play a big role in starting those relationships'.

Sharing information about children is difficult and many practitioners find themselves resorting to signing and gesturing as their only means of communication: 'So there is a lot of arm gestures and we even get to the point where we have to send notes home for a neighbour to read to the parents, which is not really very good practice'.

In order to get an understanding of what this perspective was I interviewed four English mothers who have young children attending total immersion settings in Munich, Germany. All four felt that the acquisition of a second language was a good thing and in fact one mother talked about how she hoped this would help her boys when they returned to England, because they would be attending schools in Wales where they would have to learn the Welsh language. In line with research that suggests that children who are exposed to a second language early in life have a propensity for language learning she felt that the transition to Welsh would be made easier. All of the mothers said that they had no problems with their children's emotional development as a result of attending a German Krippe, because they felt that as their children attended before they were fluent in their native language they were almost on a level basis with their non-speaking German peers:

> because it was the start of learning English if you like, their native tongue, and then they were bringing in this second language at the same time, alongside it really.

> Neither of them could talk when they went so they haven't really had those communication issues.

One mother, however, did relate the following anecdote about a friend's child, which is further evidence of the importance of the children attending the setting as early as possible in order for there to be no impact on their emotional well-being or the way in which they establish relationships with the other children:

> one little boy out here who's like 'Mummy, I don't want to go to nursery, they don't understand me', so that's quite hard, but I think, with them being that little bit younger, that perhaps helped my boys.

Two of the mothers added that there were issues about the second language acquisition if there were large numbers of children attending with the same mother tongue:

> so her first year she was completely on her own as an English speaker, second year, we've got a new girl, and she is, same age as Oscar and Nancy, and Nancy actually, spends more time with the English than the German as a result of her coming into the class.

For the other mother the issue of a common language is compounded by the fact that her girls are twins. When I talked to her she raised the issue of twin language (which I will discuss later in more detail) and how, now that the girls are fluent in German, they rarely use this personal language but that, when they are playing, they speak to each other in German. Have they dropped their own personal communication because having acquired German as a second language, which neither of their parents speak, they can use this as their 'secret language'? This mother talks about how when her girls first attended the Krippe she asked that adults focused on the girls' acquisition of German:

> One of the teachers spoke very good English, but I said from the outset I think it's great that you can speak English and for me if there's any wires crossed it's good that we can communicate with one another, but on a day to day basis I'd like you to speak German to the girls … I'd say it took the first six months for them to really get the hang of things and understand, but I think they learnt a lot of the language through play interaction and watching the children, and association, so it would be you know, a child was playing with a puppet, a doll, but that word would come naturally because that word was used all the time.

When looking into the mother's comments about her twin daughters' 'private language' it is important to distinguish this parental perspective from the research. The research seems to suggest that the reasoning behind the secret language all revolves around the language development of multiple-birth children. As Dodd and McEvoy (1994, p. 273) suggest, although 'twin language' can appear common, there have been no findings that 'support the claim that multiple birth children use an autonomous language'. What does appear from the research is that often with multiple-birth children the language is immature and so, because they spend so much of their time together, twins are able to understand one another (just as many parents can understand their children whilst others cannot) and it appears as if they are talking in their own language.

As Thorpe (2006, p. 392) explains:

> The evidence from studies of twin children's communications and parent report together indicate that:
>
> 1. A small group of twin children have a unique and exclusive communication which is predictive of poorer language.
>
> 2. Many twin children, by virtue of their shared social context and close relationship, are better able to interpret each other's immature speech and so may appear to have a 'twin language' based on shared understanding.

Questions for reflection

If you have twins in your setting discuss how you feel their language is developing in relation to their peers. Could this be a good reason for not having twins in the same environment in order to challenge their language development?

When I talked to the mothers about their children using German at home they all said that this was something that only really seemed to happen once the children were older; this is in line with what the practitioners also stated when they were talking about code-switching:

> At Krippe they'd get a little bit mixed up, so they'd asked for something and then they'd say 'danke', just little odd words and things but now they can see there's a clear difference … they seem to say, well at home I speak English, and we speak German in a Kindergarten.

All of the mothers included in this small scale research study viewed their child's acquisition of a second language as a positive thing for their child's general overall development. What was interesting, however, was their view of what implications there were for their children on returning to the UK. Most of the mothers felt that their child would settle in well but they often talked about their children perhaps not being ready for school. This ironically is in contrast to what Sir Michael Wilshaw (2014, p. 9) regards as the tools that young children need when they enter education in the reception class – what is known as school readiness:

> This concept of school readiness has been boiled down into 'Ten ticks' that parents can understand and relate to. These ticks are the basic skills that are felt to equip children for their start within the formal education system.

- To sit still and listen
- To be aware of other children
- To understand the word 'no' and the boundaries it sets for behaviour
- To understand the word 'stop' and that such a phrase might be used to prevent danger
- To be toilet-trained and be able to go to the loo
- To recognise their own name
- To speak to an adult to ask for help
- To be able to take off their coat and put on shoes
- To talk in sentences
- To open and enjoy a book

Having met these children I would regard them all as 'ready for school' using the above criteria. This is not to diminish the worries of those parents who may still have concerns similar to the following mother:

> The difference between Kindergarten and this school in particular, the school doesn't do the national curriculum but they have a timetable for the day, again it's very basic, but, they do introduce basic maths, English, the alphabet

and those things aren't covered in a Kindergarten its pure play, well learning still but through play, very much like the Kinderkrippe, so, I don't know, I think as a parent you have this fear that they're going to be behind slightly when we go back to England.

Code-switching

Another aspect of acquiring language which is of interest is the way in which some children code-switch, which means using words from the different languages in the same sentence.

Meisel (1994) makes a distinction between code-mixing, which occurs in very young children acquiring two languages, and code-switching, which occurs when the child has a strong understanding of their native language. The practitioners who were interviewed or responded to the questionnaire also commented that when the children were confident with their native language then code-switching occurred more frequently.

Meisel (1994, pp. 415–18) echoes this opinion when he argues that children are able to use code-switching as early as age two to two-and-a-half, though grammatical knowledge is a necessary prerequisite. This would fit in with the practitioners' statements about children's confidence in their native and second language.

The following case study is a response from one practitioner which illustrates how code-switching happens in her setting.

Case study

I find that the older children in the Kindergarten (five, six year olds) are quite good at switching from German to English, but they don't tend to do this amongst each other in the group, only when speaking to English-speaking adults. The children who are being raised bilingually at home code-switch more. I hear lots of 'Denglisch' [Deutsch/German-English] sentences and phrases in the under three group and some of the children make the same 'mistakes' no matter how often they are (inexplicitly) corrected, for example I hear a lot of 'I want it not' in English which comes from 'Ich will es nicht' in German and the children seem to take a long time to be able to use 'don't' and 'I don't want it' even if they can understand it when I say it or when we look at books together, etc. The children sometimes seem to try to code-switch and speak to me in English, but this usually ends up in a Denglisch sentence with German and English words, for example today a two-and-a-half

> year old girl (English mother, German father) wanted me to help her to mash her potatoes and said 'Kannst Du please meine Kartoffeln mash it up?' and another (American mother, German father) said 'can you meine Jacke upzippern?', she made up the word 'upzippern' from 'zip it up' and added a typical ending from a German verb.

Many children code-switch because they may not yet distinguish one language from another or else they may not know the appropriate word to express themselves in one language. In Malta children are taught in both English and Maltese, with an emphasis on the use of the English language. One Maltese practitioner commented that Maltese adults code-switch when speaking in Maltese. She added that several parents are overheard code-switching when speaking with their young children like, for example: 'Fejn hu d-doggie?' ('Where is the dog?'). Obviously if parents are continuously code-switching when talking to their toddlers it is very likely that their children will code-switch when speaking.

Conclusion

Learning two languages and two grammars side by side would seem to be confusing for children, but it appears, as Byers-Heinlein et al. (2013, p. 204) state, that

> keeping track of two sets of rules, or changing fluidly from one set of rules or one lexical entry to another – both of which can be seen to result from switching between two languages or inhibiting one language whilst using another … does not, however, impact the basic skills that are required to first establish native language knowledge.

This chapter has seen how second language acquisition can support children's overall development in the early years, and that it should not be seen as a deficit model. It has used a small scale research study to challenge practitioners in their thinking about children who attend a setting with a different mother tongue.

Further reading

- Gopnik, A., Meltzoff, A. and Kuhl, P. (2001) *The Scientist in the Crib*. New York: Harper.

This book discusses how early learning can inform us about the mind and the way in which it develops. Of particular interest for the subject of language is the chapter entitled, 'What Children Learn about Language'.

* Watch the following video on YouTube: www.ted.com/talks/patricia_kuhl_the_linguistic_genius_of_babies#t-3754.

Here Patricia Kuhl explains her research into babies' brains which includes a close look at how babies develop language. In her research she has looked at the use of TV and audiotapes as a means to teach children a second language. You need to watch her discuss her findings to see if media has all the answers.

suited to whatever 'storying' they are doing. These are also areas where there is a lot of physical movement, again a distraction to any interaction. A quiet area therefore is not just about cosiness and comfortable furniture it is about where it is positioned. Another factor which I think is worth considering is the height of the ceilings in a room. Often settings have high ceilings which tend to make the sounds in the room echo; here what needs to be considered are ways in which the ceiling can be lowered (especially in the quiet cosy area), as this has the effect of bringing the area in and reducing the amount of echo that there is in the room. The work of Elizabeth Jarman on Communication Friendly spaces is a good starting point; use the updated 2013 version of the book to help with the development of an environment which focuses on the role of supporting, among others, speaking and listening skills (Jarman, 2013).

In a baby room one of the things that I think needs careful consideration is adult seating. In all rooms it is important that the adults have comfortable seating so that they can engage with children at their level, but in a baby room I think that there has to be some adult-sized domestic furniture (a settee for instance) so that an adult can be relaxed whilst making good eye contact with a non-mobile baby. Not only is this good practice for interaction but is also a feature of the emotional environment (Clare, 2012). I also think it is very important for the adults to be comfortable in order for them to be able to maintain an involved interest in what the baby or child is saying.

The following case study shows how for one child the opportunity to sit and share a book with an adult in a comfortable manner is very important.

Case study

This is an episode in a day nursery and shows the interaction between the practitioner and Maisie aged 14 months.

- Maisie decides that she wants to look at a book with the adult. She snuggles in and sits on the adult's knee
- As they open the book together Maisie is looking very closely and she is feeling the pages (they evidently had had a tactile book previously and Maisie obviously remembers this experience)
- Maisie is very interested in the book and she is smiling a lot as she shares the book with the adult. She responds as the adult reads to her

(Continued)

(Continued)

- Maisie indicates that she has finished one page and is ready for the next by going to turn the page over
- Maisie now begins to verbally interact by making animal sounds associated with the pictures. There was a lovely time when she stroked the picture of the dog
- Other children come and join in on the edge – this does not bother Maisie
- As the pages are turned over you can see her looking all over the page to take all of the detail in
- The adult and Maisie now start a new book – again she studies the pictures and indicates when she wants the page turning over
- Maisie is very happy and content on the adult's knee
- She gets up after a while carrying the book around with her

This episode lasted just a few minutes but you can see that Maisie is using her experiences to make links and also that her emotional well-being is high.

If we take a further look at communication spaces for babies, the changing area is of great importance. In a busy baby or toddler room it is often very difficult to have a one to one interaction in a personalised manner. The changing area gives the practitioner the perfect opportunity for this interaction to take place. I always remember as the mother of three children under three-and-a-half years of age how difficult it was to have a special interaction with my youngest child; I found that I was afforded this opportunity when I was changing her nappy. She became the main focus of my attention. It is therefore imperative that the changing area be given some attention with regard to communication. Practitioners need to ask themselves whether or not they can engage in a meaningful interaction in this area.

Does this space:

- Create an atmosphere of calm?
- Mean that adult and child can make good eye contact?
- Allow for an unrushed interaction?
- Have other resources (for example mobiles) with which adult and child can interact?

Another area of a setting which should encourage interaction is the outdoor environment. Obviously here it is difficult to monitor the noise levels of our busy environments; depending on where the setting is located there are many external factors which impact on a listening environment. These could be traffic, neighbouring schools and aeroplanes among others. Despite this the outdoor environment should be one that is conducive to interaction. Practitioners can make use of external noises by getting children to lie down, close their eyes and listen. This will hone children's ability to differentiate between sounds – a skill that is needed when they have to segment words into their different component parts (DfES, 2007).

What is needed in the outdoor environment is a space where children can explore and investigate and where they can use language to talk about their discoveries. The following case study demonstrates one such discussion and shows how one small incident can have an impact on a child who has always been a reluctant talker.

Case study

The children of a playgroup are accessing the outdoor environment. This area is not large and is completely laid to a concrete surface but the adults have tried to ensure that the children have a valuable experience when they are outside. Where the concrete meets the park fencing a boy has made a discovery which has excited him: a slug. An adult has gone to investigate what his excitement is about and taking advantage of the situation she (bravely) picks up the slug and she and the boy talk about the slug and what they can see. The child is involved and animated as he asks the adult if he can hold the slug.

This interaction continued for some time with the child telling the adult what it felt like. This did not stop at the playgroup; the next day the boy's mother reported that all the way home he was excitedly chatting about the slug and was keen to get into his own garden to discover some more.

What is also needed in the outdoor environment, which can be loud and frantic with children running and bikes racing round, is a space where once again children can be reflective and where they can sit with their friends and chat. This space can be a den, a tent, a willow arbour or just a mat on the grass.

Case study

In one setting that I visited the children were lucky enough to have access to a forest school site on their premises. Within this area there was a garden shed. This was a lovely space; the adult had put curtains up and was using upturned wooden crates as seats. It was winter and the children came into the garden shed as a group at the end of the session to talk about what they had been doing that morning. The adult closed the curtains and the children sat on the upturned crates. First on the agenda was a mug of hot chocolate; the atmosphere was complete and the children, feeling warm and cosy, sat in an environment which encouraged them to talk about their adventures.

When looking at both the indoor and outdoor environments it is important that the experiences that are on offer to the children are relevant and meaningful. Many settings that I visit just take the indoors outside; what is needed are experiences which are relevant to the environment. For instance, outdoor role play would not be a kitchen (except of course unless it is a mud kitchen) but rather a barbeque, picnic or camp fire. Books outside would not be story books but rather factual books which children can use to help them discover more about the natural world.

One aspect of challenging children's language development within the environment which is worth considering is to look at how children are grouped. Research from the Millennium Cohort study (Mathers and Sylva, 2007) and the Neighbourhood Nurseries Initiative (Mathers et al., 2007) has shown that when older children were present in a room, there was a better quality of interactions. If you consider the Vygotskian theory of the Zone of Proximal Development (ZPD) (1978), where children have their learning scaffolded by more experienced others, having children of mixed age groups not only supports their emotional well-being, but the older children can act as language models within the continuous provision (Clare, 2012). Although some research suggests that when care is offered in mixed age groups this can have an impact on the emotional behaviours of younger children (Mathers et al., 2007).

Print-rich environments and displays

When we consider an environment for the development of communication, language and literacy we often talk about having print-rich environments, but what does this mean? Does it mean that every square inch of the room needs to be covered in writing? I have seen a nursery classroom where the writing of the children was displayed on the ceiling! If we are to have what is considered a print-rich environment then like everything else this needs to be meaningful. What we need to think about is what is relevant to the particular groups of children; for me an alphabet frieze is meaningless in a baby room. What we need here are things that babies are familiar with – pictures of objects which they can point to so that the adult can name or comment on them.

The best possible display to evoke conversation or visual interaction is the use of a family space. This is a collection of photographs bought in from the children's homes displayed at a child's height, which they can point to and, for older children, discuss. Not only is this an opportunity for interaction but it is also an opportunity to support babies and young children with their emotional well-being. One of the barriers that practitioners always mention when I advocate this space is that parents don't bring the photographs in. I think here it is a case of emphasising for parents the importance of this display; make them aware when they register that this is to help their child to settle, to give them a sense of belonging and a starting point for a conversation with a key adult. This display is useful for the adult as it gives a joint topic of interest to talk about – an ice breaker. The case study of the adult within the environment with Maisie below is another example of how an ice breaker can help children.

When we consider the amount of print that children engage with within their community it is important that we reflect this within our environments. If we reflect back on the point raised earlier in this book, we will see that one of the child's first interests in the written or printed word is their name. Children are egocentric so we need to make sure that they have the opportunity to see their name throughout the environment. Not only does a child's name on their drawer, on their coat peg and on their pictures give a child a sense of belonging and good emotional well-being, it also gives them an opportunity to engage with the written word; one which is meaningful to them.

Although it is a given nowadays I think it is important to remind practitioners that displays and the associated writing should be visible to the child. I still see displays that are meant for children but which are so high that children cannot talk about or interact with them. If a display is for a child it should be visible to them, it should be well organised; words and labels should not be lost in a myriad of colours which detract from the meaning of the display. As Barton and Brophy-Herb (2006, p. 32) remind us, 'exposure to print-rich environments, with many opportunities to see, make, read and hear how words are shapes [that] are central in the world of grown-ups, enhances the motivation and learning of emergent literacy skills'.

Within a print-rich environment it is important to make use of environmental print; this can be defined as 'words and symbols found in everyday life such as signs, advertising and product packaging' (Brock and Rankin, 2008, p. 120). Everywhere that we go in our lives there are either symbols or words telling us what to do or what something is. We have already seen how children easily engage with the digital symbols in our society; the same goes for the written word. From when they wake in the morning and choose their breakfast cereal, children are exposed to print, and it is through this exposure that they begin to make links. Oscar's favourite cereal at the moment is 'the O cereal' (Cheerios); he makes this link of the round-shaped cereal to the start of his name. What practitioners need to do is make use of environmental print by reflecting this within their environments.

Resources within the continuous provision

Once the environment has been established it is important then to see what resources are being offered within it to help children develop their communication, language and literacy skills through their child-initiated play. This is easy when you consider areas such as mark making and book areas but perhaps a little more difficult or even 'forced' in other areas. What I mean by 'forced' is that sometimes in our drive to demonstrate that children can develop these skills, the resources we place in the areas somehow look out of place. For example, in a role play area, in an endeavour to demonstrate that children have access to environmental print, empty bottles of washing-up liquid or cereal boxes are added, not small ones but the large sizes we would use at home; they look out of place because they are too large. Other times the role play area is themed and adults will tell you this to help the children develop and extend their vocabulary and language when imitating real life in this area. This is not a bad thing as long as the theme comes within the children's scope of experience. Frequently I see travel agent themes, when I would suggest that very few children have this experience as holidays are now booked online at home; I see greengrocers, butchers and florists when actually children shop with their parents in the large supermarket. What we need to do is give children the opportunity to develop vocabulary through experiences – through things that they know and can relate to.

Questions for reflection

- How often do we adapt the resources and areas according to the individual needs or preferences of children? For example, how many of us consider putting an area on the floor for boys to engage in mark making? We might add clipboards (frequently offered without paper and or a pencil!) but do we clear a space on top of the units for children to write standing up?
- Do we look at the different schemas that children may be demonstrating and then adapt the resources in the environment accordingly? Even if children are not showing us that they are in a schema do the resources in the areas mean that children who are in a schema can follow this independently within the continuous provision? A good example of how this can be done is in Nutbrown's 4th edition of *Threads of Thinking* (2011) in relation to how stories can reflect children's different schematic play (pp. 112–13).

The adult role within the environment

The adult is the key to how babies and young children will interact independently and with others within the environment. Firstly, it is the adult who has planned and created the environment to promote and provide opportunities for children to develop their communication, language and literacy skills. We have already seen the importance of the adult role in modelling and narrating whilst engaging with babies and young children. Another link to this is the way in which the adult uses opportunities within the environment to interact with children. The following case study illustrates how an effective adult uses Maisie's actions to engage her with words. Maisie is 20 months old at this time.

Case study

- The adult moves into the room as she is going to feed a baby. When she starts to feed the baby she is talking to her gently about what she is going to do. Maisie stands watching for a while before moving to

(Continued)

(Continued)

stand next to the adult to see what is going on. The adult suggests that she goes to put her blanket away in one of the drawers. This idea appeals to Maisie and she moves towards the drawers. She begins to pull the drawers out, looking for the right one. She perseveres and stands on tip toes to look inside the box to see if it is the right one and if there is any room in it

- Eventually Maisie decides on one and tries to push the blanket inside – because the drawer is at a higher level she is unable to push the whole of the blanket in and so she just lets it fall out again. She picks it up and tries again
- The adult who has been observing Maisie's progress suggests that she pulls the drawer out onto the floor and then put the blanket in. Maisie does this and is successful in achieving her goal
- Maisie now turns her attention to pushing the drawer back in. The adult is giving her encouragement but Maisie is looking at the adult and not where the drawer should be going and as a consequence can't align it properly. With further encouragement and suggestions to look at where the drawer is going, she succeeds

As you can see the adult here has not planned this interaction; it occurs naturally and spontaneously and we can clearly see that Maisie understands; she has comprehension. She can carry out instructions and the adult in this scenario is demonstrating elements of Vygotsky's ZPD in that she is moving Maisie onto another level of understanding.

Activity

Consider the ways in which the adults in the room use and observe the opportunities to engage in interaction with babies and young children during the routines of the day.

Observation of children's communication can throw light upon a child's development in other areas of learning. The following case study shows how in fact a child's excellent language skills mask her social development.

Case study

I was visiting and observing children in a nursery school. No children were targeted for the observations; this was about how children were involved in the environment and how good their well-being levels were (Laevers, 1994). I chose to observe a girl in the role play area; she was sitting at the table and there were a number of other girls playing there.

At first I was impressed by the girl's levels of language; she spoke clearly, with good use of vocabulary. In the area of Communication and Language outcomes she would have scored highly. I would say that she was involved in what she was doing, but after a few minutes I thought that there was something missing. As she was talking I had wrongly assumed that she was interacting with the other children in the area but it soon became clear that the other children were not part of this conversation and that in fact there was no interaction.

When I discussed this later with the teacher it appeared that the girl was achieving high outcomes across the board except within social interaction; for some reason she didn't 'fit in' with the other children. We decided that perhaps this was because she had no shared interest with the other children; her family life and experiences were not the same as the others. The teacher decided to talk to her mother; she came up with what I consider to be an innovative and successful way of overcoming this problem. She explained that, although not a fan herself, a number of the other girls were interested in Peppa Pig, and although not a particular advocate of recommending TV as a solution she asked the mother to let the girl watch the programme so that she had a common interest with the other children. This proved to be a highly successful strategy. If you consider how, as adults, we sometimes use books, TV or music to engage with new acquaintances to 'break the ice', you can see how we also use this strategy in our everyday lives.

Questions for reflection

How often in your observations do you look at the wider picture; not just focusing on the outcome that you think is being observed/ assessed? Do you observe in a holistic manner or do you find that in this outcome-driven atmosphere that sometimes you miss things that are happening in the classroom?

When I deliver training to practitioners about their role in supporting and developing children's communication and interaction I begin by asking them to consider the following four words: *Interfere, Intervene, Interrupt, Interact*. These are words we use all of the time but if we are to consider them in relation to our practice with babies and young children we need to start with some definitions:

- **Interfering** – unwanted, unwarranted or unnecessary intrusion
- **Intervening** – to involve oneself in a situation so as to alter or hinder an action or development
- **Interrupting** – to stop (a person) in the midst of doing or saying something, especially by an interjected remark
- **Interaction** – a mutual or reciprocal action

What we need to do is to consider which of these we actually do within our practice. I would suggest that a lot of our time is spent interfering, intervening and interrupting, because we tend to do these things naturally; whereas with interaction we are more considered, and perhaps less natural, when we interact because it is this that marks us out as good practitioners. Perhaps like me you struggle to …

- always to remember to ask open-ended questions
- prevent yourself from interrupting because you think you are helping
- stop intervening before an interaction between children gets 'out of hand', when sometimes it is better for them to find the words for themselves to solve the problem
- remember that children don't always want to involve you in their play; sometimes we are just *not* wanted

If we can get past this then what we need to reflect on is what our interactions look like. The following is a list of ways in which we should approach our interactions with babies and young children:

- Listening
- Gesturing
- Expression
- Questioning
- Imagining
- Reflecting
- Explaining
- Posing problems

- Wondering
- Talking

The way in which adults interact with children and the quality of these interactions has been the focus of research (Murray et al., 2006) which has shown that children from higher socio-economic status (SES) homes are at an advantage in the quantity of positive language that they are exposed to at home, compared to those from less advantaged backgrounds. It also informs us that, 'Despite differences in quantity, the children in high quality child care were being exposed to the same quality of language that was found in the high SES homes' (Murray et al., 2006, p. 236).

Activity

Look at Arnett's (1989) Caregiver Interaction Scale as an alternative method for assessing the way in which you interact with the children (see the Appendix at the end of this chapter). This scale has been used in studies such as *The Quality of Group Childcare Settings Used by 3–4 Year Old Children in Sure Start Local Programme Areas and the Relationship with Child Outcomes* (Melhuish et al., 2010), where the scales are described as:

a rating scale made up of 26 items each describing a characteristic of an interaction. The observer completes the scale by indicating how much the item relates to the observed interaction (1=not at all, 2=somewhat, 3=quite a bit, 4=very much). The items form four subscales: Positive Relationship, Punitiveness, Permissiveness and Detachment. (p. 6)

Conclusion

Communication and interaction are the key to children's future learning; without these skills children will struggle in their education and within their social lives. In order for children to succeed we need to concentrate on getting these right before assessing young children's ability to read and write. It is our duty as early years practitioners to help babies and young children reach their potential and to support parents by making them informed about good practice.

Recently I was listening to a radio programme and one of the contributors said the written word is more emotive than the printed word. In the words of Maya Angelou (1970), 'Words mean more than what is set down on paper. It takes the human voice to infuse them with shades of deeper meaning.' This is what we want for the children in our care, to be able to *infuse* words so that they can express what they truly think and feel.

Further reading

- Nutbrown, C. (2011) *Threads of Thinking*, 4th edition. London: Sage Publications.

In this fourth edition of *Threads of Thinking* Cathy Nutbrown writes about how to put the theory of schemas into practice. Of particular interest are Chapters 6 and 7, which focus on 'Patterns of Literacy' and 'Supporting Children's Thinking through Stories'.

Appendix: Arnett's (1989) Caregiver Interaction Scale

Table 7.1

CAREGIVER INTERACTION SCALE INSTRUCTIONS
(Arnett 1989)

GENERAL
Circle one score far each item after observing in the setting for at least 2 hours.
• Be sure to note examples of behaviors on your score sheets as you see them during the observation to make rating more accurate. • When scoring, it may help to think of the word "true" at the end of each rating descriptor (e.g., not at all *true*, somewhat *true*). • Because the words "somewhat and "quite a bit" may sound very similar to some people, here's some help, Think of "not at all" and "very much" as representing the 2 endpoints of a continuum, with "somewhat" and "quite a bit" as points equidistant between the 2 ends.
Item 4. Interpret this item to mean that the teacher places an overly strong focus on obedience. If the teacher values obedience a normal amount or less, the score is "1." If you believe that she values obedience more than normal, then you must decide whether it's somewhat high, quite a bit high, or very much high.
Item 7. Interpret "misbehavior" very broadly; for example, a rule can be explained if children want to take off their shoes and the caregiver says no. If there are absolutely no such incidences during the observation, you may score this item as "Not Applicable."
Item 8. To credit the teacher for this, you must hear the teacher say something to encourage children to try something new. Just placing new, interesting materials in the classroom is not enough. "New experiences" should be interpreted broadly to include things like reading a new book, playing a new game, etc.

Item 9. It may help to remember that this item is measuring whether the teacher is *too* permissive. If you believe the teacher uses a normal amount of control (or even uses too much control), then the score is "1." If you believe that the teacher is too permissive, then you must decide whether it's "somewhat," "quite a bit," or "very much" too permissive.

Item 15. It may help to remember that this item measures the teacher's permissiveness. Although the word "reprimand" may have negative connotations, do not interpret it negatively. If the teacher intervenes when children misbehave, then the score is "1." If you do not observe any misbehavior (broadly interpreted, see clarifications to item 7), score this item "1." If you see children misbehaving without any intervention from the teacher, then you need to decide whether she "sometimes," "quite a bit," or "very much" doesn't reprimand children when they misbehave.

Item 17. If you do not observe any punishment during the observation, you should score this item as a "1."

Item 19. Pro-social behavior includes behavior toward adults and other children.

Item 23. If the teacher provides the "right amount" of supervision (or even supervises them too closely), the score is "1." If the teacher does not supervise the children closely enough, then you must decide to what degree she does *not* supervise closely.

SCORING INSTRUCTIONS

Total Mean Score: A higher score on the total mean item score indicates "better" (more positive, appropriate) interactions. To compute the total mean (average) item score:

(1) Reverse the scores of items 2, 4, 5, 9, 10, 12, 13, 15, 17, 20, 21, 22, 23, 24 and 26. For example, if an item is scored "4" during the observation, use a score of "1" when computing the total score; if an item is scored "2" during the observation, use a score of "3" when computing total score.
(2) Sum the scores for all items (be sure to use the "reversed" scores in the sum as directed).
(3) Divide the total sum by 26 to get the total mean item score.

The total mean item score will be a number between 0 and 4.

CAREGIVER INTERACTION SCALE
(Arnett 1989)

Center Name:

Teacher Name: **Observation Date:**

Data Collector:

For instructions, clarifications and scoring, click here.	Not at all true	Somewhat true	Quite a bit true	Very much true
1. Speaks warmly to the children.	1	2	3	4
2. Seems critical of the children.	1	2	3	4
3. Listens attentively when children speak to him/her.	1	2	3	4
4. Places high value on obedience. More	1	2	3	4
5. Seems distant or detached from children.	1	2	3	4
6. Seems to enjoy the children.	1	2	3	4
7. When the children misbehave, explains the reason or the rule they are breaking. More	1	2	3	4

(Continued)

Table 7.1   (Continued)

8. Encourages the children to try new experiences. More	1	2	3	4
9. Doesn't try to exercise too much control over the children. More	1	2	3	4
10. Speaks with irritation or hostility to the children.	1	2	3	4
11. Seems enthusiastic about the children's activities and efforts.	1	2	3	4
12. Threatens children in trying to control them.	1	2	3	4
13. Spends considerable time in activity not involving interaction with the children.	1	2	3	4
14. Pays positive attention to the children as individuals.	1	2	3	4
15. Doesn't reprimand children when they misbehave. More	1	2	3	4
16. Talks to the children without explanation.	1	2	3	4
17. Punishes the children without explanation. More	1	2	3	4
18. Exercises firmness when necessary.	1	2	3	4
19. Encourages children to exhibit prosocial behavior, e.g., sharing, helping. More	1	2	3	4
20. Finds fault easily with children.	1	2	3	4
21. Doesn't seem interested in the children's activities.	1	2	3	4
22. Seems to prohibit many of the things the children want to do.	1	2	3	4
23. Doesn't supervise the children very closely. More	1	2	3	4
24. Expects the children to exercise self-control: e.g., to be undisruptive for group provider-led activities, to be able to stand in line calmly.	1	2	3	4
25. When talking to children, kneels, bends or sits at their level to establish better eye contact.	1	2	3	4
26. Seems unnecessarily harsh when scolding or prohibiting children.	1	2	3	4

Source: www.eec.state.ma.us/docs1/qris/20110121_arnett_scale.pdf

References

Aldridge, M. and Waddon, A. (1995) 'What do parents expect? Children's language acquisition in a bilingual community', *Language Awareness*, 4 (4): 203–20, doi: 10.1080/09658416.1995.9959884 (accessed 04/08/2014).

Alexander, R. (2009) *Children, their World, their Education: Final Report and Recommendations of the Cambridge Primary Review*. Abingdon: Routledge.

Allen, G. (2011) *Early Intervention: The Next Steps*, http://preventionaction.org/sites/all/files/Early%20intervention%20report.pdf (accessed 23/01/2015).

Allen, G. and Duncan-Smith, I. (2008) *Early Intervention: Good Parents, Great Kids, Better Citizens*, www.centreforsocialjustice.org.uk/UserStorage/pdf/Pdf%20reports/EarlyInterventionFirstEdition.pdf.

Angelou, M. (1970) *I Know Why the Caged Bird Sings*. New York: Random House.

Arnett, J. (1989) *Caregiver Interaction Scale*. Unpublished rating scale, www.eec.state.ma.us/docs1/qris/20110121_arnett_scale.pdf.

Barton, L. and Brophy-Herb, H. (2006) 'Developmental foundations for language and literacy from birth to 3 years'. In Rosenkoetter, S. and Knapp-Philo, J. (eds) *Learning to Read the World*. Washington DC: Zero to Three, pp. 15–60.

Blaiklock, K. (2013) 'Talking with children when using prams while shopping', *NZ Research in Early Childhood Education Journal*, 16: 15–28.

Bourke, L. and Adams, A. (2011) 'Is it difference in language skills and working memory that account for girls being better at writing than boys?', *Journal of Writing Research*, 3 (3): 249–77.

Bowlby, J. (1989) *The Making and Breaking of Affectional Bonds*. Oxon: Routledge.

Bradford, H. and Wyse, D. (2013) 'Writing and writers: the perceptions of young children and their parents', *Early Years: An International Research Journal*, 33 (3): 252–65, doi: 10.1080/09575146.2012.744957.

Brock, A. and Rankin, C. (2008) *Communication, Language and Literacy from Birth to Five*. London: Sage Publications.

Bronfenbrenner, U. (1979) *The Ecology of Human Development: Experiments by Nature and Design*. London: Harvard University Press.

Brown, R. and Hanlon, C. (1970) 'Derivational complexity and order of acquisition in child speech'. In Brown, R. (ed.) *Psycholinguistics*. New York: Free Press.

Byers-Heinlein, K., Burns, T. and Werker, J. (2010) 'The roots of bilingualism in newborns', *Psychological Science*, 21: 343–8.

Byers-Heinlein, K., Fennell, C. and Werker, J. (2013) 'The development of associative word learning in monolingual and bilingual infants', *Bilingualism: Language and Cognition*, 16: 198–205, doi:10.1017/S1366728912000417 (accessed 12/06/2014).

Carle, E. (2010) *The Bad Tempered Ladybird*. London: Puffin.

Chaucer, Geoffrey and Coghill, N. (2003) *The Canterbury Tales*. London: Penguin.

Chomsky, N. (2003) *On Nature and Language*. Cambridge: Cambridge University Press.

Clare, A. (2012) *Creating a Learning Environment for Babies and Toddlers*. London: Sage Publications.

Cocozza, P. (2014) 'Are iPads and tablets bad for young children?', *Guardian*, 8 January 2014, www.theguardian.com/society/2014/jan/08/are-tablet-computers-bad-young-children (accessed 12/01/2015).

Conteh, J. (2012) *Teaching Bilingual and EAL Learners in Primary Schools*. London: Sage Publications.

Crystal, D. (2011) *A Little Book of Language*. New Haven and London: Yale University Press.

David, T., Goouch, K., Powell, S. and Abbott, L. (2003) *Birth to Three Matters: A Review of the Literature*. Nottingham: DfES Publications.

DCSF (2008a) *Curriculum Guidance for the Foundation Stage*. Nottingham: DCSF Publications.

DCSF (2008b) *Every Child a Talker: Guidance for Early Language Lead Practitioners*. Nottingham: DCSF Publications.

DCSF (2008c) *Statutory Framework for the Early Years Foundation Stage*. Nottingham: DCSF Publications, http://webarchive.nationalarchives.gov.uk/201005 12134444/http://nationalstrategies.standards.dcsf.gov.uk.

DfE (2012a) *Foundations for Quality. The Independent Review of Early Education and Childcare Qualifications. Final Report*, www.gov.uk/government/uploads/system/uploads/attachment_8789udata/file/175463/Nutbrown-Review.pdf.

DfE (2012b) *Statutory Framework for the Early Years Foundation Stage*. Nottingham: DCSF Publications.

DfE (2013a) *More Great Childcare. Raising Quality and Giving Parents More Choice*, www.gov.uk/government/uploads/system/uploads/attachment_data/file/219660/More_20Great_20Childcare_20v2.pdf (accessed 27/05/2014).

DfE (2013b) *Early Years Outcomes*, www.gov.uk/government/uploads/system/uploads/attachment_data/file/237249/Early_Years_Outcomes.pdf.

DfE (2014a) *Statutory Framework for the Early Years Foundation Stage*. Nottingham: DCSF Publications.

DfE (2014b) *Early Years Foundation Stage Handbook*, www.gov.uk/government/ uploads/system/uploads/attachment_data/file/301256/2014_EYFS_handbook. pdf (accessed 21/04/15).

DfE (2014c) *The EYFS Progress Check at Age Two*, www.gov.uk/government/ uploads/system/uploads/attachment_data/file/175311/EYFS_-_know_how_ materials.pdf (accessed 21/04/15).

DfES (2000) *Curriculum Guidance for the Foundation Stage*, Nottingham: DCSF Publications, http://webarchive.nationalarchives.gov.uk/20100512134444/http:// nationalstrategies.standards.dcsf.gov.uk.

DfES (2002) *Birth to Three Matters*. Nottingham: DfES Publications.

DfES (2005) *Communication Matters*. Nottingham: DfES Publications.

DfES (2007) *Letters and Sounds: Principles and Practice of High Quality Phonics*. Nottingham: DfES Publications.

Dodd, B. and McEvoy, S. (1994) 'Twin language or phonological disorder?', *Journal of Child Language*, 21: 273–89, doi:10.1017/S0305000900009272 (accessed 01/08/2014).

Early Education (2012) *Development Matters*. London: British Association for Early Childhood Education.

Elliott, E.M. and Olliff, C.B. (2008) 'Developmentally appropriate emergent literacy activities for young children: adapting the early literacy and learning model', *Early Childhood Education Journal*, 35: 551–6, doi: 10.1007/s10643-007-0232-1.

Farrant, B.M. and Zubrick, S.R. (2012) 'Early vocabulary development: the importance of joint attention and parent–child book reading', *First Language*, 32: 343–64, originally published online 18 October 2011, doi: 10.1177/0142723711422626 (accessed 13/05/2014).

Fennell, C., Byers-Heinlein, K. and Werker, J. (2007) 'Using speech sounds to guide word learning: the case of bilingual infants', *Child Development*, 78 (5): 1510–25.

Field, F. (2010) *The Foundation Years: Preventing Poor Children Becoming Poor Adults*. London: Cabinet Office.

Fonagy, P. (2001) *Attachment Theory and Psychoanalysis*. New York: Other Press.

Fox, A.V., Dodd, B. and Howard, D. (2002) 'Risk factors for speech disorders in children', *International Journal of Language and Communication Disorders*, 37 (2): 117–31.

Gopnik, A., Meltzoff, A. and Kuhl, P. (1999) *How Babies Think*. London: Phoenix.

Gopnik, A., Meltzoff, A. and Kuhl, P. (2001) *The Scientist in the Crib: What Early Learning Tells Us about the Mind*. New York: Harper.

Guardian (2013) www.theguardian.com/money/2013/jan/29/childcare-reform-pro-posals-fierce-criticism (accessed 27/05/2014).

Hall, K. (2003) *Listening to Stephen Read: Multiple Perspectives on Literacy*. Buckingham: Open University Press.

Hansard (2013) www.publications.parliament.uk/pa/cm201314/cmhansrd/ cm131203/debtext/131203-0001.htm#13120350000001.

Harms, T., Clifford, R.M. and Cryer, D. (2003) *Infant/Toddler Environmental Rating Scale Revised (ITERS-R)*. New York: Teachers College Press.

Honig, A. (2001) *Teaching Our Children to Read*. Thousand Oaks, CA: Corwin Press.

Jarman, E. (2013) *The Communication Friendly Spaces Approach*. Ashford: Elizabeth Jarman Ltd, www.elizabethjarmantraining.co.uk (accessed 09/06/2014).

Jopling, M., Whitmarsh, J. and Hadfield, M. (2013) 'The challenges of evaluation: assessing Early Talk's impact on speech language and communication practice in children's centres', *International Journal of Early Years Education*, 21 (1): 70–84, doi: 10.1080/09669760.2013.771324.

Kimura, L. (2006) 'Music: the great organizer for early language and literacy'. In Rosenkoetter, S.E. and Knapp-Philo, J. (eds) *Learning to Read the World*. Washington DC: Zero to Three.

Kuhl, P. (2004). 'Early language acquisition: cracking the speech code'. *Nature Reviews: Neuroscience*, 5: 831–43.

Kuhl, P. (2010) *The Linguistic Genius of Babies*, www.ted.com/talks/patricia_kuhl_the_linguistic_genius_of_babies#t-3754 (accessed 10/06/2014).

Laevers, F. (1994) *The Innovative Project Experiential Education*. Leuven: Centre for Experiential Education.

Leach, P. (2010) *The Essential First Year: What Babies Need Parents to Know*. London: Dorling Kindersley.

Leach, P. (2011) 'The EYFS and the real foundations of children's early years'. In House, R. (ed.) *Too Much, Too Soon*. Gloucestershire: Hawthorn Press.

Lenneberg, E.H. (1967) *Biological Foundations of Language*. New York: Wiley.

Levy, R. (2009) '"You have to understand words … but not read them": young children becoming readers in a digital age', *Journal of Research in Reading*, 32 (1): 75–91, doi: 10.1111/j.1467-9817.2008.01382.x.

Macrory, G. (2010) 'Language development: what do early years practitioners need to know?', *Early Years: An International Research Journal*, 21 (1): 33–40, doi: 10.1080/09575140123296 (accessed 02/05/2014).

Mashburn, A.J. (2008) 'Quality of social and physical environments in preschools and children's development of academic, language, and literacy skills', *Applied Developmental Science*, 12 (3): 113–27, Business Source Premier, EBSCO*host* (accessed 22/01/2015).

Mathers, S. and Sylva, K. (2007). *National Evaluation of the Neighbourhood Nurseries Initiative: The Relationship between Quality and Children's Behavioural Development*. Nottingham: DfES Publications.

Mathers, S., Sylva, K. and Joshi, H. (2007) *The Quality of Childcare Settings in the Millennium Cohort Study*. Nottingham: DfES Publications.

Meisel, J.M. (1994) 'Code-switching in young bilingual children', *Studies in Second Language Acquisition*, 16: 413–39, doi: 10.1017/S0272263100013449 (accessed 01/08/2014).

Melhuish, E., Belsky, J., MacPherson, K. and Cullis, A. (2010) *The Quality of Group Childcare Settings Used by 3–4 Year Old Children in Sure Start Local Programme Areas and the Relationship with Child Outcomes*. London: DfE Publications.

Michael-Luna, S. (2013) 'What linguistically diverse parents know and how it can help early childhood educators: a case study of a dual language preschool community'. *Early Childhood Education Journal*, 41: 447–55, doi: 10.1007/s10643-013-0574-9 (accessed 01/08/2014).

Mueller, V., Sepulveda, A. and Rodriguez, S. (2013) 'The effects of Baby Sign training on child development', *Early Child Development and Care*, 184: 1178–91.

Murray, A.D., Fees, B.S., Crowe, L.K., Murphy, M.E. and Henriksen, A.L. (2006) 'The language environment of toddlers in center-based care versus home settings', *Early Childhood Education Journal*, 34 (3): 233–9, doi: 10.1007/s10643-006-0138-3 (accessed 08/08/2014).

Murray, L. and Andrews, L. (2000) *The Social Baby*. Richmond: CP Publishing.

Neumann, M. (2014) 'An examination of touch screen tablets and emergent literacy in Australian pre-school children', *Australian Journal of Education*, 58 (2): 10922, doi: 10.1177/0004944114523368.

Notari-Syverson, A. (2006) *Everyday Tools of Literacy*. In Rosenkoetter, S.E. and Knapp-Philo, J. (eds) *Learning to Read the World*. Washington DC: Zero to Three.

Nutbrown, C. (2011) *Threads of Thinking,* 4th edition. London: Sage Publications.

Nutbrown, C. (2013) *Shaking the Foundations of Quality*, www.shef.ac.uk/polop-oly_fs/1.263201!/file/Shakingthefoundationsofquality.pdf.

OECD (2012) *Starting Strong 111: A Quality Toolbox for Early Childhood Education and Care*. Paris: OECD Publishing.

OECD (2014) 'A profile of student performance in reading', in PISA 2012 Results: What Students Know and Can Do (Volume I, Revised edition, February 2014): *Student Performance in Mathematics, Reading and Science*. Paris: OECD Publishing, www. keepeek.com/Digital-Asset-Management/oecd/education/pisa-2012-results-what-students-know-and-can-do-volume-i-revised-edition-february-2014_9789264208780-en#page1.

Partanen, E., Kujala, T., Tervaniemi, M. and Huotilainen, M. (2013) 'Prenatal music exposure induces long-term neural effects', *PLoS ONE* 8 (10): e78946, doi: 10.1371/journal.pone.0078946.

Partridge, H.A. (2004) 'Helping parents make the most of shared book reading', *Early Childhood Education Journal*, 32 (1): 25–30.

Renfrew, C. (2010) *Action Picture Test Revised Edition (The Renfrew Language Scales)*. London: Speechmark Publishing Ltd.

Roberts, R. (2010) *Wellbeing from Birth*. London: Sage Publications.

Robinson, M. (2003) *From Birth to One: The Year of Opportunity*. Buckingham: Open University Press.

Rose, J. (2006) *Independent Review of the Teaching of Early Reading: Final Report*. Nottingham: DfES Publications.

Rueda, R. and Stillman, J. (2012) 'The 21st century teacher: a cultural perspective', *Journal of Teacher Education*, 63: 245–53.

Rutter, M. (1972) *Maternal Deprivation Reassessed*. Harmondsworth: Penguin.

Saxton, M. (2010) *Child Language*. London: Sage Publications.

Schickedanz, J. (1999) *Much More than the ABC's*. Washington DC: National Association for the Education of Young Children.

Siegal, M., Surian, L., Matsuo, A., Geraci, A., Iozzi, L., et al. (2010) 'Bilingualism accentuates children's conversational understanding', *PLoS ONE*, 5 (2): e9004, doi:10.1371/journal.pone.0009004. www.signalong.org.uk/methodology/index. htm (accessed 21/04/15).

Snow, C.E. (1977) 'The development of conversation between mothers and babies', *Journal of Child Language*, 4: 1–22, doi:10.1017/S0305000900000453 (accessed 13/05/2014).

Stern, D. (1991) *Diary of a Baby*. New York: Basic Books.

Stern, D. (1998) *The Birth of a Mother*. New York: Basic Books.

Sylva, K., Meluish, E., Sammons, P., Siraj-Blatchford, I., Taggart, B. and Elliot, K. (2003) *The Effective Provision of Pre-School Education (EPPE) Project: Findings from the Pre-School Period (Research Brief No: RBX15-03)*. London: DfES Publications.

Thorpe, K. (2006) 'Twin children's language development'. *Early Human Development*, 82: 387–95.

Tickell, C. (2011) *The Early Years Foundation for Life, Health and Learning*, www.gov.uk/government/uploads/system/uploads/attachment_data/file/180919/DFE-00177-2011.pdf.

Trevarthen, C. and Malloch, S. (2000) 'The dance of wellbeing: defining the musical therapeutic effect', *Nordisk Tidsskrift for Musikkterapi*, 9 (2): 3–17.

Truss, E. (2014) www.gov.uk/government/speeches/elizabeth-truss-speaks-about-early-years-teachers.

Vygotsky, L. (1978) *Mind in Society: The Development of Higher Psychological Processes*. London: Harvard University Press.

Whitmarsh, J., Jopling, M. and Hadfield, M. (2011) *I CAN's Early Talk Programme: Independent Evaluation of the Impact of Early Talk on Addressing Speech, Communication and Language Needs in Sure Start Children's Centre Settings*. University of Wolverhampton and DFE.

Wilshaw, M. (2014) *Unsure start: HMCI's Early Years Annual Report 2012/13 speech*. http://webarchive.nationalarchives.gov.uk/20141124154759/http://www.ofsted.gov.uk/sites/default/files/documents/about-ofsted/speeches/Early%20Years%20Annual%20Report%201213%20-%20Unsure%20start%20-%20HMCI%20speech.pdf (accessed 04/08/2014).

Yamada-Rice, D. (2010) 'Beyond words: an enquiry into children's home visual communication practices', *Journal of Early Childhood Literacy*, 10 (3): 341–63.

Index